Marian,
from Nancy + Stuart Anderson

Runnin' on Rims

Runnin' on Rims

Appalachian Profiles

Photographs and Text by
Jock Lauterer

Algonquin Books of Chapel Hill · 1986

Algonquin Books of Chapel Hill
Post Office Box 2225
Chapel Hill, North Carolina 27515–2225

Printed in Japan

Library of Congress Cataloging-in-Publication Data
Lauterer, Jock.
   Runnin' on rims.

   1. North Carolina—Social life and customs.
2. North Carolina—Biography.   3. Mountain life—
North Carolina.   4. Aged—North Carolina—
Biography.   5. Aged—North Carolina—Interviews.
I. Title.
F261.L38   1986   975.6'04'0922   85-30631
ISBN 0-912697-33-4

for Maggie

Contents

Prologue

It had been snowing for two days so that the steep-sided mountains that huddled about the little North Carolina community
of Marion looked like huge gray sleeping cats with their furry
backs turned to the wind.

The small crew that produced the two-year-old weekly *McDowell
Express* had no trouble walking to work that snowbound day—for
we had all found homes close to our Main Street office just in case
one of those unpredictable heavy snowstorms blew down out of the
Blue Ridge. Slogging through the drifting, blowing snow to work
had imbued us with a zealous sense of duty in the face of the
elements. The cozy newspaper office fairly bustled with our
enthusiasm.

But it was another matter for our volunteer contributors,
"country correspondents," like Tillie Twitty, who wrote weekly
accounts of seemingly trivial comings and goings from her outlying
neighborhood.

Tillie's column, "Ebonnaires," was especially important to us
since it was the only regular reportage we carried from the small
black community. As editor in chief, I had come to prize Tillie's
innate ability at turning a neat phrase. The woman had a definite
way with words, and she added considerably to our newspaper's
local flavor.

So we were all a little anxious on that winter press-day when the
deadline drew near and still no column had arrived from Tillie.
The typesetter too was growing nervous because "Ebonnaires" always took longer to set than normal copy; she didn't look forward
to deciphering Tillie's enthusiastically bounding handwriting.

At last, when it seemed we couldn't hold the space a minute longer, in came Tillie—puffing and blowing. Stamping the snow off her feet, she waved her limp copy overhead like a victorious cavalry flag.

When I asked her what her problem had been, Tillie started in, "Well, Mr. Jock," and went on, trying to catch her breath, "I was coming down the road and had a flat tire." She shook her head. "Got out to change it, and Lord, the spare it was flat too! Then while I was setting there wondering what I was going to do, another tire went flat on me right there." She wagged her head again.

"No kidding? So how'd you make it to town?" I wondered aloud, surrounded now by several staffers who sensed a good story brewing.

"Well, Mr. Jock," she replied, grinning ruefully, "I come in just runnin' on rims. Yeah! Runnin' on rims."

And so the expression was born. How many times since then have I found myself emotionally, financially, or creatively running on rims? And yet I would still feel resilient largely because of Tillie Twitty and all the many other generous mountain people who by their example had taught me how to get along with good cheer and a sense of well-being in spite of any obstacles.

It seems significant that none of the people I interviewed ever complained about their station in life or their lack of worldly goods. They had learned early a great lesson and their whole lives reflected that practical ideal: if you're out of something, either grow it or make it yourself; if you want something you can't afford, do without—or better yet, improvise.

I have to think of Reid Biddix repairing his Model A with baling wire and chewing tobacco; of Ernest Edwards making a photographic enlarger out of a broken camera and a stovepipe; and of J. Lewis Hardin at his family's hundred-year-old country store where the glass counters were so cracked from age that they were riveted together with bolts and J. Lewis's handmade wooden washers. Those counters bore the warning: "Don't lay on me please—I been here a long time."

There is humor here, to be sure. But it is the kind of good cheer reflecting a bedrock of solid, time-tested values undergirding a deep well of collective folk humor. I couldn't help but be impressed with how it buoyed those people up and seemed to have the power of exorcising despair. One could do much worse than "run on rims."

When I started collecting these folk stories in 1969, the purpose was purely functional and for the present. I was a young, undefined writer-photographer working on newspapers in the mountains of western North Carolina. Doing human profiles seemed to be my specialty. The vision of what I was doing, and what it was my privilege to be a part of came to me slowly, like Kurt Vonnegut's proverbial bubble rising in the the Prell bottle. The notion that I was collecting oral history and that it might be a profoundly important function practically had to bludgeon its way through to my consciousness.

By 1973, I had enlisted enthusiastically in the "back to the land" movement, a groundswell that venerated all things rural. This I was able to do in my professional as well as personal life. Seeking a suitably lofty label for my work, I came up with "folkloric photojournalism," a rather unwieldy but grandiose-sounding term of my own proud invention.

Meanwhile, a four-year saga of building a log home served to draw me closer in spirit to the land and people of the North Carolina hill country. When the cabin was done in 1978, so too was my first book, a collection of interviews and photographs whose mission was mainly one of preservation, similar in intent but not in form to the *Foxfire* books (started not so coincidentally also in the late sixties).

I chronicled thirty-two old masters of plain living in *Wouldn't Take Nothin' for My Journey Now*, published in 1980 by the University of North Carolina Press. That book, whose title comes from an old gospel song, drew upon my experiences in Rutherford County, where from 1969 to 1980 I was co-editor of *This Week*, a weekly newspaper I had helped to found. There I met legions of native humanists and humorists who, though they may have lacked for material comforts by modern standards, were rich in values, spirit, and a personal sense of well-being.

Laughably, after all these years I still can't come up with a better term for my brand of oral history than folkloric photojournalism. "Folk" works because my people were for the most part native, indigenously rural, and not self-conscious of how different they were from the rest of our zany society.

"Folklore" appeals to me because much of what I was being told was the verbal legacy—the lore—of their clan and country.

"Photojournalism," a two-headed monster of a word, fits because it suggests to me that the collector is both writer and photographer.

When in 1980 I moved higher into the mountains and started another weekly in Marion (McDowell County), N.C., I soon realized I was well on my way to forming a second collection of the people I'd encountered. Subsequently, a year as editor of *Mountain Living* magazine based in Black Mountain, N.C., allowed me to expand the anthology to include folks from the higher mountain counties of Buncombe, Avery, Watauga, Polk, and Mitchell.

As I look at a relief map of North Carolina and examine the far western side, I'm struck again with how the mountains always remind me of a rug summarily scrunched into a corner—as if its owners were having a party and were in a hurry to clear the floor for dancing: all the soft ridges and valleys rising and falling, running and folding in a repetitious, parallel northeast to southwest direction.

Little wonder that the early white settlers coming from the east and north in the late eighteenth century considered the old Smokies a formidable obstacle. Looking at the Southern Appalachians from the air, you have to wonder—how did those people get up and across those ramparts with only primitive trails and ox-drawn wagons? And what kind of people would attempt such a passage, or want to hack out a mean existence in such a high, remote, and lonesome place? And surely the people who live there today must retain much of the remarkable spirit and grit of their trailblazing forebears.

I found myself drawn to the old people of the region who, for the most part, were the hardy remnant of those Scots-Irish and German pioneers who had settled the coves and hollows hundreds of years before. The majority of my work was with people over eighty who vividly recalled an age before electronic mass communication, motor vehicles, manned flight, telephones, electricity, paved roads, or indoor plumbing—much less personal home computers. Without wishing to romanticize them or to make them seem "quaint," I felt compelled to record their stories and photograph with respect their fine lined faces.

I attended apple-butter makings, 'coon hound water races, hog killings, and country dances. I visited with the likes of Emmett Gray who lived with bears; counted myself a friend to the generous, Zorba-like Christmas tree grower, Joe Henson; and relished my time with Howard McKinney, who refused to own a car because he preferred Pearl and Nancy, his mules. I met Aunt Kate Burnette, who at eighty-six insisted on cutting all her own cookstove firewood by herself; and the Biddix family who lived so far back up in Turkey Cove that they only came out in their black Model A Ford once a week for supplies—and that was only if Armstrong Creek wasn't on the rise—because they had to drive through the axle-deep rushing waters in the old car.

That "my people" (as I came to think of them) didn't possess what has been called "media savvy" required that I develop my own home-grown style of interviewing. It was much as if I were Alan Lomax collecting folk songs in the thirties. I approached my people with as much patience and respect as an archaeologist on a dig, rather than like a typical deadline-driven, daily newspaper reporter—which, of necessity, I have been from time to time.

The first factor I had in my favor was that most folks knew of me through the newspaper, so they were familiar with my work, and knew they would be treated fairly in print. That, and the fact that after a certain time I was considered an insider and not just some city-slicker flatlander, worked to my advantage.

The keys to my approach were time and consideration. I made every attempt to "dis-interview," which is to say nurture the atmosphere of a social visit, rather than that of a formal interview. I always came to my people, talking to them wherever they were the most comfortable, preferably while they were doing something. If, for instance, it was Aunt Kate Burnette, we would be chatting while she sawed firewood for her cookstove.

I eschewed many of the trappings of my trade: no tape recorder at all because I instinctively felt that electronic thing would have threatened and intimidated most of these people. I kept my notepad and cameras well out of sight for the first part of the visit, while the preliminary talk of weather, children, and gardens went apace. Only when I couldn't stand it a second longer, the notepad would come out—and even then, notes were taken in my higgledy-piggledy shorthand, while I made sure to keep eye contact as much as possible, often covering the fact that I was still writing after they were finished with a sentence by responding verbally as I continued to scribble. It's not an easy way to conduct an interview, but it worked for me.

The camera, a most alarming piece of equipment to most

people—rural or otherwise—didn't make its appearance until the visit was hours' old and the subject and I had established respect, friendship, and rapport. Only when I felt it was just right did the Nikon come out of the bag. The secret I found was to envision the picture I wanted before I sort of absently picked up the camera, acting as if it were no big deal but rather something just as natural as scratching my head. I would shoot quickly and keep talking while keeping eye contact with the subject. That requires the photographer to keep both eyes open and not to hide his face behind the camera. Often I'd be talking and shooting at the same time. Then I might put down the camera and chat for another five minutes before picking it up again for another brief shooting session.

My style was to defuse the potential intensity of the interview with my sincere affection. If done right, the social encounter of the *visit* was paramount in the mind of my old person, while the professional result I was seeking became secondary. Thus, I came to earn the trust of my people so I could go back for subsequent "visits" as I needed.

I never used a motor-drive (photographer Darryl Heikes says we already have enough Machine Gun Kellys) or a flash—for the same reason I avoided tape recorders. In a home heated just by the fireplace, where they didn't have a phone, all that electronic brouhaha would have been spiritually out of sync with the setting and totally disruptive and distracting to my people.

Following the "non-interview" I would rush back to my vintage black Royal (so old, the keys were illegible) and try to decipher my note-taking. The folk stories were all written in accurate dialect in order to faithfully reproduce the essence of the encounter. My intent was to try to capture a specific present—what John Szarkowski, director of the photography department of the Museum of Modern Art, calls "a concise segment in the temporal chain." Thus the stories are all pie slices of these peoples' lifetimes. This collection makes no claim of being a definitive study. Rather, it is a celebration of the self, a "fanfare for the common man," a bouquet of vignettes.

I've also taken the liberty of including two other people in this collection who, though not native to the mountains, have become acculturated to the region and who have wonderful stories that beg preserving: Caribbean-born jazzman Isidore Langlois who played the guitar with Fats Waller and most of the other greats of Harlem in the thirties; and Johnny-Appleseed-Come-Lately, Harold M. Clark, who devoted his entire life to nurturing his laurel seedlings and carrying them from the West Coast to the Southern Appalachians.

Without quite realizing it, I turned into a field gerontologist. Interviewing hundreds of old people began to afford me with a broad overview of how mountain people coped with aging. If I had distributed and collated a questionnaire on well-being to my old people, they would have laughed and said they'd known all along the requirements for a long, happy life—as described by Dr. Robert N. Butler, chairman of the department of geriatrics and adult development at the Mount Sinai Medical Center in New York. In his introduction to the book *How a Man Ages* (Ballantine, 1984), Dr. Butler states: "It is important to have a social network of good friends and acquaintances who can sustain us in times of crisis, especially in times of loss and grief. We must also have a sense of purpose beyond our occupation—a passion, something that guides us—be it a love of baseball, a grandchild, books, or civic activity. It is wise, too, to have a balanced portfolio of interests: if one loves music but becomes deaf, it helps to have something else to turn to."

I find it no coincidence that every single one of my old people *did* something, be it manual—like the guitarmaker J. D. McCormick, or centenarian John McCall who still gardened—or civic—like scoutmaster Walter Earley or senior citizen center songleader "Pop" Gourley. If nothing else, they were actively involved with the unsung art of "re-collecting" their memories of their lifetimes. And that very process of sharing their remembrances with me often had a profound impact on them.

How we age and the effects of aging are coming under increased scrutiny as the baby boomers approach senior status. Curtis Pesman, author of *How a Man Ages*, estimates that since the proportion of elderly in the United States keeps rising each year, eventually millions of us will be part of an unprecedented "*gray boom*."

Dr. Butler advises: "No longer can we afford to view older people as aliens, strange interlopers from a strange land. We are likely to enter that land ourselves, and we would do well to prepare for it."

Daniel Levinson, author of the groundbreaking ten-year study *The Seasons of a Man's Life* (Random House, 1978), agrees that our culture's myopic focus on the joys of being and staying young have shortchanged our collective perspective on aging. Levinson writes: "The connotations of youth are vitality, growth, mastery, the heroic; whereas old age connotes vulnerability, withering, ending, the brink of nothingness. Our overly negative imagery of old age adds greatly to the burden."

The flowering of powers I witnessed in my old mountain people supports the latest findings and thinking on the subject of aging. Dr. Butler concludes that aging is not simply a downhill course, that we *do* continue to grow and develop, with judgment, experience, and creativity expanding throughout our lifetimes.

The ingredients of graceful, productive aging as related to me by these folk are as natural and free-form as Aunt Lena Dellinger's biscuits. "Nannie" would shake her head and smile kindly when citified grandchildren yearning for precise measurements and specific ingredients demanded to know how she made them so light and puffy. "Why Law', child, it's just a liddlebit of this and a liddlebit of that," she would say, as if echoing a sampler hanging in her bedroom: "The greatest truths are the simplest."

I left the mountains in 1983 to return to my hometown and teach journalism at the University of North Carolina at Chapel Hill. My great friend and adopted mountain pappy, J. D. McCormick, tried to convince me it was a terrible mistake. That's J. D. on the cover with one of his handmade guitars. He planned to record a country music hit that would make so much money that he'd be able to buy me another newspaper back in those hills. "I'll be settin' on a stump, just a-waitin' for you, honey," the old mountain man grinned toothlessly, and laughed at the notion.

It was also J. D. who taught me another great lesson: "Nothin' don't come from nothin'." He ought to know, for J. D.—and the rest of my old friends whose lifetimes lie between these covers—may all be "runnin' on rims," but they do it with such a style and grace that it endears them to us. May their legacy be indelible.

JOCK LAUTERER
Chapel Hill, N.C.
July 1985

C·13876·G
OHIO 1956
EN·327
C·13876·G
7015

•DRIVE SAFELY•
H·99
62 NORTH CAROLINA
•DRIVE SAFELY•
WT·240
61 NORTH CAROLINA
•DRIVE SAFELY•
8226·SW
61 NORTH CAROLINA
•DRIVE SAFELY•
YH·8828
62 NORTH CAROLINA
•DRIVE SAFELY•
4172·RC
62 FARM·TRUCK N.C.
•DRIVE SAFELY•
HB·265
62 NORTH CAROLINA
MORGANTON N.C.
•DRIVE SAFELY•
SB·607
NORTH CAROLINA 60
•DRIVE SAFELY•
7896·SW
61 NORTH CAROLINA
•DRIVE SAFELY•
3305·SU
61 NORTH CAROLINA
•DRIVE SAFELY•
NL·232
62 NORTH CAROLINA
ARIZ 65
7407
TLR. ACC.
RC TEX 04-65
S30390
FARM TRUCK N.C. 63
8722RB

*Every man beareth the whole stamp of the human
condition.*

—Montaigne

*It's a mark of life: the wrinkles, after all. It depends on
how they fall; it depends on how people have been living.
After a certain age you've got the face you deserve.*

—Henri Cartier-Bresson

Nothin' don't come from nothin'.

—J. D. McCormick

Part One

Making Things . . .
Doing Things

*I built twenty-one [guitars] and burnt three. . . . I was burnin'
some trash in a barrel out back and had one of them guitars—just
stuck it in that trash fire. I had to. It wadn't no count! Wouldn't
play right—and I didn't want nobody to have it if it had my
name on it.*

—J. D. McCormick

J. D. McCormick, Guitarmaker

They ain't nobody like me . . .

J. D. McCormick, sixty-two, loved to laugh. When something
struck him as funny, the laugh seemed to start at his scuffed
brogans and travel up his body like ripples in a pond, shaking his
suspendered midsection, jangling his pocket-watch fob and chain
musically, bobbing his adam's apple over his top-buttoned shirt,
until the laugh got to his face where it burst out of his generous,
toothless mouth: "Haw-Haw!" J. D. let it loose like a trumpet
fanfare.

Seated on the front porch swing of the weatherboarded log
house, J. D. had thrown both arms over his head and whooped a
greeting when he had spotted the visitor coming up the rutted trail
to his McDowell County home there in the hollow.

"Come on up hyar and set a spell and I'll give you the best of my
life that I can," he proclaimed. J. D.'s face was a study constantly
alternating between mock seriousness and flights of comic fancy, a
face of an old snapping turtle accompanied by a growling gravel pit
of a voice.

On his lap he cradled a guitar, a golden-faced beauty with a dis-
tinctive star-and-half-moon pick guard. He rested upon it gently
the way a man stands with one arm affectionately clinging around
his best girl's curving waist.

"I was born a cornmiller's son. Daddy he ran Silver's mill on
Crooked Creek. He was a cornmiller till the day he died.

With the song over,
J. D. McCormick erupts into laughter.

A guitar takes shape in J. D.'s workshop.

"I ran the mill from the time I was fourteen till I was twenty-one. Daddy'd run it all day and I'd work it at night. It was a big ol' water mill. Torn down and gone now. Had wooden gears. People nowdays won't believe mills had wooden gears. Shoot! Wood'll last for hundreds of years." J. D. spat tobacco juice off the porch and squinted into memory.

"Used to grease them gears with taller. Y'know—taller: that's lamb's grease. Many a time I remember Daddy holler, 'Jay!'—he called me Jay—'Run down there and grease them gears! It's a-hollerin'.' And I'd do it, and after a while it'd quieten down . . . haw-haw!" J. D. let that laugh go again.

"I guess I got into tradin' that way too. I've seen 'em when the millyard'd be fulla mule and horse-drawn wagons, sometimes four or six mule teams—all just a-waitin' to have wheat, corn, or rye milled. And they'd spend the night sometimes and the boys and men'd pass the time swappin' pocketknives and such. I've seen 'em swap *mules* too, right there in Daddy's millyard." J. D. rared back, eyes wide at the remembrance of such an awesome transaction.

Music was always a part of his life. He was a guitar and banjo player back before "things got awful tough in what we called the Hoover Days. Used to eat a lot of 'Hoover ham.' Why, you know what that was, don't you? Fatback!"

J. D. remembered sadly how when he lost a thumb and forefinger from his left hand in a sawmill accident, "Mama cried for two days. She'd just go around in circles a-weepin', 'He won't git to play me no more songs.'

"But I meant to keep on playin' the guitar and banjo, so I just learned myself how to chord it with what I had," J. D. declared, popping his faded, gray suspenders for emphasis over his olive-green workshirt.

From his dad he'd learned blacksmithing, and he combined that with his natural ability as a woodworker to become an instrument maker. After years of trial and error J. D. taught himself how to make his own guitars. "I built twenty-one and burnt three," he said matter-of-factly. "I was burnin' some trash in a barrel out back and had one of them guitars. . . . Just stuck it in that trash fire—I *had* to. It wadn't no count! Wouldn't play right—and I didn't want nobody to have it if it had my name on it," he glowered.

Those guitars that survived their maker's trial by fire are collector's items. "The inside's mahogany. It's got a rosewood back and side, a walnut neck, rosewood fingerboard and bridge, and the inlay is plastic odds and ends I pick up at the steakhouse. And if people want to know a price—tell 'em it's priceless.

"Some folks think you're gonna reach up in the blue sky and grab a fortune. . . . Well, it took God six days and *He's* the Almighty. And even then, after six days, He said, 'I'm *tahred*.'" J. D. grimaced and then laughed, "Haw-haw! Nothin' don't come from nothin'."

J. D. roused himself from his porchside perch and led the way to his "music room," a large, low-ceilinged back bedroom crammed with antique recording equipment and musical instruments. "It's all piled up in here, honey," he apologized. "Used to transcribe radio shows in here for the Farm Hour with Reid Wilson on the Saturday Night Round-Up. That was on WWNC in Asheville. Our family played. Called it the J. Douglas Country Show."

The music that went out of that little log cabin back up on Crooked Creek was unabashedly country, and J. D. was proud of it. "I like bluegrass all right. But country's what I am and country's what I sing. I come up with Gene Autry. He was my main man—my fantasy, y'understand. I'd learn his songs as quick as they come out; him and Jimmy Rodgers."

J. D. was working on a new master tape containing eight of his songs he said he intended to take to Nashville. "I don't care nothin' about being famous—just give me that *money.*" He paused for effect, then came the explosive laugh like a big rock dropped into a deep pool.

"To write a song, y'gotta have an idea," he resumed studiously. "I was comin' back from Nashville one time when I got this one idea for a song: I was drivin' along and I saw this big ol' mountain man comin' outa the woods. He had a beard on him and his woman walkin' behind him, y'know, an' I come home and got to scratchin' on that song." J. D.'s heavy-lidded eyes shone with satisfaction as he switched on the tape machine and the tune came thumping out of the old speakers:

> I'm just an ol' mountain man,
> Don't know no modern ways of livin',
> All I know is an ol' woodstove
> And an ol' iron skillet . . .

As the last line of the chorus echoed around the room—"Smoky Mountain ways / Are good enough for me"—he grinned hugely. "Y'orta play it again. Every time you hear it you'll like it a little more."

Shaking back his head J. D. laughed again. "Well, one thing's for sure—I'm just an ol' mountain man. They ain't nobody like me—they can't be. Haw-haw!"

At the shop's door,
J. D. pauses to reflect on
a life of country music.

A shy smile ignites the face of proud Model-A owner Reid Biddix
as he takes the old car out for a spin.

Reid Biddix and His Model A

Hit just don't seem like home 'lessen that ol' car's settin' out there.

The steep-sided valley, like a cup formed by hands, fell away abruptly to the center crease where rain-swollen Armstrong Creek thrashed its noisy way through Turkey Cove.

A muddy trail appeared to end there at the log footbridge, but continued over a rock-bottomed ford across the wide creek. There it emerged and wound past a frieze of apple trees holding sway beside a humble homestead in the hollow. The twin-rutted path then made a beeline to a corncrib with a lean-to shed sheltering a goggle-eyed black beauty—a vehicle that most folks see only in automotive museums or in old movies.

The 1931 Model A Ford had been the Biddix family car for over forty years—and Reid Biddix, seventy-four, plainly adored it. Sitting by a pitted Sunny Jim woodstove with his younger sister Dollie and brother Edward, Reid concluded in his gentle but firm way of talking, "Hit'll wear out a new one—for hit's made outa real stuff. Real metal."

A warm rain was drumming tentative fingers on the tin roof of the weatherboarded farmhouse. Reid rubbed his leathery hands together in front of the stove, recollecting how he got the car. "I bought it back in the time of the German 'n' Jap war. I had run up on a fella who was being drafted. I'd already been turned down. He said he'd bring it out to me to see if I liked it. Well, I waited

"

when it was time for him to come and one of 'em—my brothers—
said, 'I don't believe your man's a-comin'.' But just as they said that,
here he comed—and his car was as good as his word."

Reid had worn out one motor, put another in, and didn't see any
reason why the Model A shouldn't keep right on humming. "Hit's
needing painting—and I ain't even washed it this whole winter. But
we just did put in a new muffler on it, me 'n' Phillip, my brother.
Got it from an antique place outa Gastonia."

Reid learned to drive as a boy, but he was so short for his age
that he had to stand on the seat to see out of the windshield. "Back
then, all you had to have was a license, and there wasn't no age
limit. The patrol used to come through every other day from
Spruce Pine and it cost a dollar. I just sat there by the road one
day till the patrol came by and I got mine. That was before the
days of insurance. Now, some people depend on that insurance too
much. It sure won't save a fella's life.

"I rid with one fella up the mountain one time and I could see
he was taking a right smart of the road. He said, 'Let's see if our
insurance works.' But I just went a little piece and got out. I could
see he was taking too much road on people.

"That reminds me of the time I was coming off Little Switzerland
without any brakes." Reid was warming to his subject. "I just had
first and reverse and no brakes. When I got home my brother
asked me how I got home alive," the soft-spoken ridgerunner
chuckled to himself. "Well I just put it in first and any time I went
to going too fast, I'd just lightly touch reverse and that'd hold it
back. Just push the reverse pedal in light, y'know, so's it wouldn't
strip it. Them A Models you had to drive mostly with your feet
anyway."

The worst experience Reid ever had in his car was the time he
was sideswiped by a schoolbus. Though he couldn't remember the
date of the fracas, he knew it was before the days of mandatory
automotive liability insurance. "I was a-dreadin' that schoolbus because that boy he driv reckless. Well, here he come, right at me. A
rock face on one side and nothin' on t'other. I thought he was
gonna hit me center. Boy, if he had, it'd a-been too bad and that's
all. But I swerved and that bus, why hit stood on two wheels as we
passed. If he'd had kids I believe it'd a-throwed 'em through the
window—but he was empty. Well, it caught my left fender and
bent it plumb back to the hood. Boy, it jarred us up. It costed him

Past the apple trees and down the loamy trail to Armstrong Creek,
Reid steers the black beauty.

twenty dollars and they fired him. But it'd a-been too late if'n he'd
a-been carrying any kids."

Reid took a book of cigarette papers out of one of the many
pockets of his Red Camel overalls. Cupping one sheet between
thumb and forefinger, he poured a deposit of Prince Albert into
the crimped paper. A methodical lick sealed the hand-rolled cigarette—and with a scratch of an Ohio Blue Tip match the tobacco
flared to life. "We go to town once a week. For groceries," he said,
exhaling.

"But I have to watch the creek. It's fed from the top of the Blue
Ridge and it'll rise in a hurry. I have a rock I always look at. If it
wets that rock then I'd better keep out with my car. I'm plumb
afraid to try it then. I might drown'er out and get adrift. It'd be
easy to turn one over."

Gas prices concerned the Biddixes. Sitting by the window, Dollie lamented, "Hit's gettin' so poor folks can't hardly make it." But Reid was encouraging. "My car they say it's pretty light on gas. If it wasn't, we'd be in for it. A fella I know has a great big heavy car—a gas-drinker I call 'em. Can't hardly even keep it gassed up.

"I put two gallons in mine last week. That makes twelve miles here to Marion and twelve miles back, and I put two gallons back in this week. That's pretty good for reg'lar gas, ain't it?"

Reid said inspections weren't any trouble, even though the '31 Ford didn't come equipped with such modern amenities as turn signals. "Hit don't differ if it's snowing or raining—you still gotta poke your hand out and make those hand signals."

Hoisting himself out of his stove-side chair, he invited, "Y'wanna ride?" He donned his jacket and hat, and ambled out into the dewy rain. There under the shed roof, the old car with its bug-eyed headlamps watched Reid expectantly.

He climbed expertly under the low-hanging roof and into the faded, red-upholstered cab. Inside it was weathered but immaculately kept. The only bit of frivolity was a vintage forties clear plastic gearshift knob depicting a frizzy-haired blonde pin-up girl in a two-piece bathing suit.

Reid, with his shy but proud little smile, pushed the footstarter and the engine turned three times, then thrummed to life. A satisfied, toothy grin grew wider on the face of the car's owner. Grabbing the pin-up girl gearshift knob, he thrust her into first. Then, bending over the steering wheel, which he grasped with both hands, Reid let his old car out onto the loamy road.

Together they went bumping gently past the apple trees, the cornstubble field, woodshed, and outhouse; past brother Willie chopping wood in the drizzle; past the old German shepherd that had lost one foot in a bear trap years ago; and so down to the rolling waters of Armstrong Creek.

Stopping short of the frothing creek, Reid observed sagely that his marker rock was about covered. So the ride was abbreviated, and angling about-face, he steered the Model A back across the farm road, his hat bill thrown back in the wind and a beatific smile on his old, lined face.

Once the car was properly stabled by the corncrib, Reid headed for the fire's warmth. He doffed his coat and hat as Willie stamped in with a load of freshly split red oak. Outside one of the dogs whined piteously to be let in.

The old car rests beneath
apple tree and corncrib.

From the window they could all see the old Model A with its gay yellow wheel spokes resting in the stall. Reid admitted that he once almost gave leave to his senses and sold it for a newer model—but somehow he had never gotten around to it. And now, the car was "fifty years old and still a-runnin'," Reid declared. Practically a member of the family, he was thinking.

Dollie, still in her chair by the window, gazed out the rain-streaked pane and concluded, "Hit just don't seem like home 'lessen that ol' car's settin' out there."

WALTER B EARLEY
BOY SCOUTS OF AMERICA
PHILMONT SCOUT RANCH CIMARRON N.M.

Walter Earley, Scoutmaster

Scouting picks a feller up.

"**30** Million Scouts Since 1910," read the decal on the front door of Walter Earley's place in Marion. "One Lives Here."

Nothing could be more accurately said about seventy-eight-year-old Walter Earley, who, though he wasn't a Scout back in 1914 when he was a boy, had made up for it in his old age. For the last twenty-two years he had led Marion's Troop 209 with the honest savvy of an old woodsman.

"Now I'm a country boy and I was learned that stuff on the farm. My daddy learned me the trees and the birds and such. I can still tell what a tree is as far as I can see it. I was learning that stuff from my youth up—they didn't have no Boy Scouts in the country." Walter scowled, his sun-burnished, lean face a study in gutter-like wrinkles that seemed designed to carry off rain water. There wasn't an ounce of fat on Walter. He looked wind-carved and rain-eroded. His Scout uniform hung on him as if on a wire clothes-hanger.

He prided himself on his rough and ready Troop 209. He had turned it into a camping outfit that could take inclement weather in its stride. "When it's too rough—that's just right for us," he said.

Walter got involved with Scouting after retiring from his carpentering. Someone asked him to join the troop committee. "Never thought nothin' about it and I didn't know nothin' about Scouting. Had no intention of getting involved."

Walter Earley,
the seventy-eight-year-old scoutmaster of Marion Troop 209,
says, "Scouting's up front . . . everything about it's good."

But when the adult leader had failed to show up for a camping trip and Walter saw how it disappointed the boys, he decided to get involved. "There was only four boys in the troop at the time, so I could could get 'em all in my station wagon at once. I took 'em to the old lime mines, and I don't believe those children had ever been off before. I told 'em to just bring their pans; that we'd have supper up in the woods. I'd gone and bought a twenty-eight-pound ham and hid it in the back of my station wagon. About supper time, here come some of the parents, sorta flustrated I guess, but we just set 'em down and served 'em up a great big ol' slab o' ham—and everybody loved it. That's how we got started off. That was 1958."

In the early sixties the West Marion Men's Club donated land and built a Scout hut for the troop. Never one to take a gift without giving something back, Walter said he and his boys pitched in. "Me 'n' the boys plumbed and wired it. Me 'n' the boys painted it. An' me 'n' the boys kept up the ground too."

Walter's troop grew. Gone were the days when they could all pile in the lanky scoutmaster's station wagon. They bought the first of six buses with money made from recycling newsprint, glass, and aluminum. The latest edition, a lime-green former schoolbus, sat in back of Walter's modest frame house awaiting the next adventure. "Why, we been all over—Philmont, New Mexico, and Colorado—as well as all around here. Been on some mighty boogery trips too. Boogery? Oh, that's when you get into snakes or yellow jackets or the like."

There was the time in the early sixties when his troop was called out one winter evening to help search for a downed airplane along the Blue Ridge Parkway. "It looked like snow, and dusk was coming on. Then it just began to pour the snow. It got so deep it was up to the boys' waists. So deep they couldn't walk in places. The other rescue fellers was in there a-huntin' *us*. But we come out of it—and everybody was glad to see us safe and sound."

Then there was the time Walter had to defend his boys from a marauding bear during an Appalachian Trail hike. "It was a-rainin' when we hit the trail and a-rainin' when we got to the top of Proctor's Bald. There was a man and his son there from Tennessee and he said, 'I sure am glad to see you. I can't get a fahr going and we been here for three days eating nothing but cold canned stuff.' I went out to get those little hair-lookin' twigs off the bottom of spruce trees. Well, as I was walking back with an armful of twigs,

Walter's gang on a hike to Catawba Falls:
not a grumpy face in the bunch.

the Hensley twins began hollerin', 'Lookit what Mr. Earley's got! Lookit what Mr. Earley's got!' and I turned around—and here come a great big ol' bear a-trottin' along behind me.

"That bear stopped outside the shelter long enough for me to get the fahr a-goin just outside. It was one of those three-sided shelters with one side wide open to anything. I told the boys, 'We'll have to fight him for our food before we leave, 'cause there ain't no runnin'. We're twenty-five miles this way and twenty-five miles that way and this food's gotta last us.'

"Kenny Melton he had a machete and I had a Scout hand-ax. So I told Kenny to hit him on the rump and I'd take the other side, and told one of the littler boys to get a flaming stick and jab it at that ol' bear when he come in the shelter. Wellsir, that bear's coming at us the whole time and me a-talkin' to the boys. He got up right to the edge of the shelter and just stopped. Oh, he's mad, his hair's all riz up.

" 'Stand your ground,' I told the boys—that ol' bear just a-lookin' at me and then at the fahr, then back at me, then back at the fahr—never at the boys—just me and the fahr." Walter said the stand-off with the bear, illuminated by just the firelight, could have gone either way. There was the bear, slobbering and swaying back and forth, snuffling and growling with indecision. There was the lanky Scoutmaster with his little ax, staring down the wild beast. And there were Walter's boys all crouched behind him, big-eyed but ready with whatever weapons they could muster.

"Then I guess the fire bluffed him, 'cause he just backed off and went back in the edge of the woods. One of the boys throwed him a loaf of bread and he climbed a tree with it, and instead of tearing into that loaf, he just opened it and ate it, one piece at a time, just as pretty as you please. We never was bothered by bears after that."

Another time they took a hike on a trail so steep that "if you let loose of one tree before you grabbed the other, you'd a-been airborne." Walter grinned. Then he remembered the "boogery time with the yellow jackets over by Fontana." "The boys had to run in circles to get their lunch et. Man, you never saw so many bees. They'd fly in a feller's mouth when they went to get a bite of sandwich. But most of the times, we have the grandest of times—yessir, yessir."

Walter believed in teaching his boys fire-building without matches. He used a handbow and an elm dowel that when twirled on the simple rope lathe could start a fire in dried grass in a matter of minutes. "It's a little bit more complicated than just rubbing two sticks together, but it's fahr-by-friction, and it's the same principle," he said. "And I can start a fahr in any weather; don't care if it's been raining for thirty days, those feathery twigs on the bottom of the spruce will never get wet clear through—and they've got rosin in 'em too.

"The first thing we try to do is learn boys to be self-sufficient in the woods. I had many of 'em come to me and not able to even cook water. We teach 'em how to cook right off. We teach 'em how to keep themselves dry in the woods. Parents generly don't learn 'em how to do those things at home.

"There was this one eleven-year-old I took camping recently and I was a-fixin' the fahr and he said, 'What's that?'

"And I said, 'Why, it's a fahr. Ain't you never seen a fahr before?'

"And he said, 'No. Whatcha gonna do with it?'

"I told him I was gonna cook our supper with it.

"'Will it burn me?' he wanted to know.

"And I told him, 'Yes it will.' But he didn't believe me. Well, the fahr was just little as it started out, so I knew it wouldn't hurt him much.

"He tried it out: stuck his hand plumb in the fahr. And he didn't have to be told a second time what fahr was good for! I couldn't imagine it—he'd never seen a blaze o' fahr!

"After fahr-building, a boy needs to know about the snakes and bugs and squirrels and birds and trees—things he ain't never seen before. He needs to know one tree from another. Now, snakes fascinates 'em to death. At first a boy'll not know a black snake from a spreadin' adder. They think they're all poisonous"—Walter smiled serenely—"but we learn 'em.

"Then we learn 'em to swim. I've had numerous boys get their one-mile-swim badge. I'd say we've had many we've learnt to swim that otherwise might never a-knowed how to swim a lick. Oh, Scouting's *up front*. It keeps abreast about things a-goin' on. Everything about it's good. It just picks a feller up. Over the years I guess I've had hunnerds of boys. Never counted. But we've touched many a boy."

Preserving the old skills,
Walter starts a fire with a bow and a twirling elm dowel.
He is amazed by boys who have "never seen a blaze o' fahr!"

"Bicycle John" Lee West had a lifelong love affair
with anything on wheels.

"Bicycle John" Lee West

*I can still handle that thing—and I'll stop the day that I think
I can't.*

$\mathbf{O}$ver the hill appeared "Bicycle John" Lee West, his white-
helmeted head bobbing down the Sandy Mush road toward
home, and his raucous red Cushman scooter going "putta-put-
put-*poop*-putta-pop" like a two-wheeled popcorn popper.

John had earned his moniker as Rutherford County's oldest and
most persistent cyclist. The eighty-year-old had been on wheels
before the Hell's Angels were in leather diapers. John had a lifelong love affair with anything on wheels; he even put wheels on his
front porch chairs.

The figure on the scooter grew closer until he pulled to the side
of the road and into his driveway. "Oh brother," exclaimed the wiry
figure. "This thing is heavy—you try pushing it," he huffed. Then
the engine conked out. "It don't sound just right," he said ana-
lytically, wheeling the creature up to the back porch. Putting down
the kick stand, John commanded, "Let's pull a chair and set in
the sun."

He rolled two ladder-back cane chairs from the living room out
onto the porch. "I put wheels on my chairs so I don't have to pick
'em up," John said proudly, plopping down in one chair with the
scooter in front of him. "Rode a bicycle thirty-two years before I
got one of these. Ha-ha-ha." He enunciated his laughter. "I had to

give up a bike 'cause I got the awful-est cramps at night I couldn't sleep and would have to get up and soak my feet in salt solution. I got tired of that bike."

The March sun had a hint of spring this morning, and the light fell softly on his white-stubbled, weathered face, with its white swatch of hair and heavy-rimmed glasses. His heavy corduroy shirt was buttoned to the neck, and the collar was turned up. He wore heavy black pants and rubber wading boots with the tops cut off.

The small figure on the faded red '57 Cushman was a common sight around the mountains. Area folks vowed they'd seen Bicycle John in Atlanta, Asheville and on the top of Mt. Mitchell, the highest point east of the Mississippi. T. C. Holland down at the Sandy Mush Crown station said that when he was up at Mt. Mitchell one summer, "I heard this put-putting and looked around and there he was, I said, 'John Lee, what you doing up here?' and he said, 'Just riding around,' like it wasn't anything."

John was from Kings Mountain but moved up to his Sandy Mush farmplace in 1964 "to be near Waters's motorcycle place. I got the Cushman from them. Oh yes, they keep it going." The people down at Waters's Honda knew him well. Proprietor Joe Waters said, "He's quite a man. I'd guess he's got 180,000 miles on that bike."

He lived alone, with the scooter serving as his only transportation. John had a drink box strapped on the back of his scooter, which enabled him to "get half a month's groceries in that big box."

John had many friends, but had his rules about visitations. He installed a cigar box beside the backdoor with paper and pencil inside for notes. Over this, John had written his instructions in pencil on the white-painted wall: "If I'm not here leave a note. There's note paper in the mailbox but leave the pencil."

And on the old well that was on the back porch, John had left this command: "Don't sit on this shelf. It has nails in it. – John Lee West." Then, out in the smokehouse that served as garage and repair shop a sign warned: "Stay out. Do You Understand. – John Lee West."

John coveted the contents of that barn. "Someone was joking with me the other day. Said I must be the richest man in the county 'cause I got a scooter and two power lawnmowers. Ha-ha-ha. But I got caught when they come out with that new law about

Sounding like a two-wheeled popcorn popper,
Bicycle John's scooter appears over the rise.

wearing helmets. I was going along down about Shelby when they
got me. Feller said, 'You're doing only one thing wrong.'

"'What's that?' I asked him—knowing what it was.

"He said, 'You need a helmet—and if you weren't an old man,
I'd lock you up right now!'" John's face crinkled with laughter as he
savored the punch line again: "'. . . lock you up right now!'"

Bicycle John's driver's license was coming up for renewal soon and
getting a new license was a matter of pride for the old cyclist. "I'm
gonna go up there to present myself. If they want to give it to me—
that's fine, but I ain't gonna study *law* no more," John vowed. "I
can still handle that thing—and I'll stop the day that I think I
can't."

PEPSI
PEPSI-COLA
PEPSI
12-28 fl.oz. bottles
no deposit no return
PEPSI-COLA

Sam "Handy" Haynes, Peanutman

I didn't want my folks to count me a lazy man.

In his own way Sam "Handy" Haynes was a self-made man.

"Uncle Raleigh Haynes built the big mills in Cliffside, Avondale, and Caroleen," Sam piped shrilly, "and my Uncle Raleigh always said, 'If'n you don't have a job—then you make you one.' Well, I made me one: sellin' peanuts." Sam stuck out his little chest.

Sam, eighty-two, became a permanent fixture around town as the bicycle-riding peanutman of Spindale. He'd been growing peanuts since 1921, but it wasn't until he was eighty-one that Sam began roasting, bagging, and selling the peanuts from a red and green cart on Main Street. "I didn't want my folks to count me a lazy man," he said with a shy smile. "So I come up here. And besides, I see my friends. Oh, I might make fifty cents a day, but that's better than not having fifty cents."

Sam made his headquarters beneath one of the shade trees in front of the Methodist Church just before Main Street takes a dogleg across the railroad tracks that split Spindale clean down the middle like a giant zipper. His peanut cart was a merry mix of Yankee ingenuity and Southern spare parts. "Made that cart myself last year. It's got a lantern under the drum there to keep the roasted peanuts warm," he explained.

Eighty-two-year-old Sam "Handy" Haynes,
the peanutman of Spindale,
awaits another customer.

Sam sat on an overturned bucket sharing the shade with appleman Perry Guffey when a car pulled up along the curbside. Sam bolted from his seat with short, eager steps, bending over as he went so as to see in the window. "How many?" he demanded. A single finger was the response. Still bent like a question mark, Sam pivoted to his peanut cart, grabbed a bag, and wheeled back to the customer, stiff and precise as a wooden doll in a German wind-up clock. After the customer drove off Sam produced a ballpoint pen from his shirt pocket and deftly banged the pen's backside on his forehead to click it open, and on a small notebook he studiously recorded the transaction. Today he had sold fourteen bags. Not bad for a Thursday, he announced sagely.

Appleman Guffey was seated on an upturned peach crate, peeling and then eating an apple with a pen knife. This he did by slicing the apple in half and then scraping the knife blade back and forth across the open apple, making sort of an instant apple sauce, which he ladled into his mouth carefully with the knife blade. Guffey watched as Sam went hobbling quickly to service another peanut customer. "That ol' man's been foolin' with peanuts a long time," he surmised. When Sam returned to his seat he said in consternation, "That feller wanted to know if I had any hot tamales, if I heard him right." He shook his head and eased down slowly to his sitting bucket.

The peanutman of Spindale was born in 1890 in Pueblo, Colorado, or as he called it, "Pebble-oh." His family lived there six months before coming to the big new mill at Cliffside where his uncle was in charge of the textile operation. Sam attended Simmons School at Ferry and went to high school–level boarding school in Westminster community north of Rutherfordton. "You know, schools have made rapid progress since I was a little boy. If I could, I'd go back and study arithmetic, history, and English, but I ain't got the time. What's that? Oh why, because *then* I'd be a smart man," Sam beamed back through his scholarly looking gold-rimmed glasses.

But Sam hadn't done poorly for himself. He and his wife had "raised seven children and I'm proud of it. One of my boys is a preacher up at Pleasant Hill this side of Morganton. Another daughter's an English teacher at Central High—Mrs. Raymond Lyles." And then there was the peanut business. "Built my own peanut roaster. Found an old oil stove I bought for two dollars.

"Handy" Haynes, grabbing another bag
for one of his regulars, asks, "You like them
peanuts I sold you pretty well?"

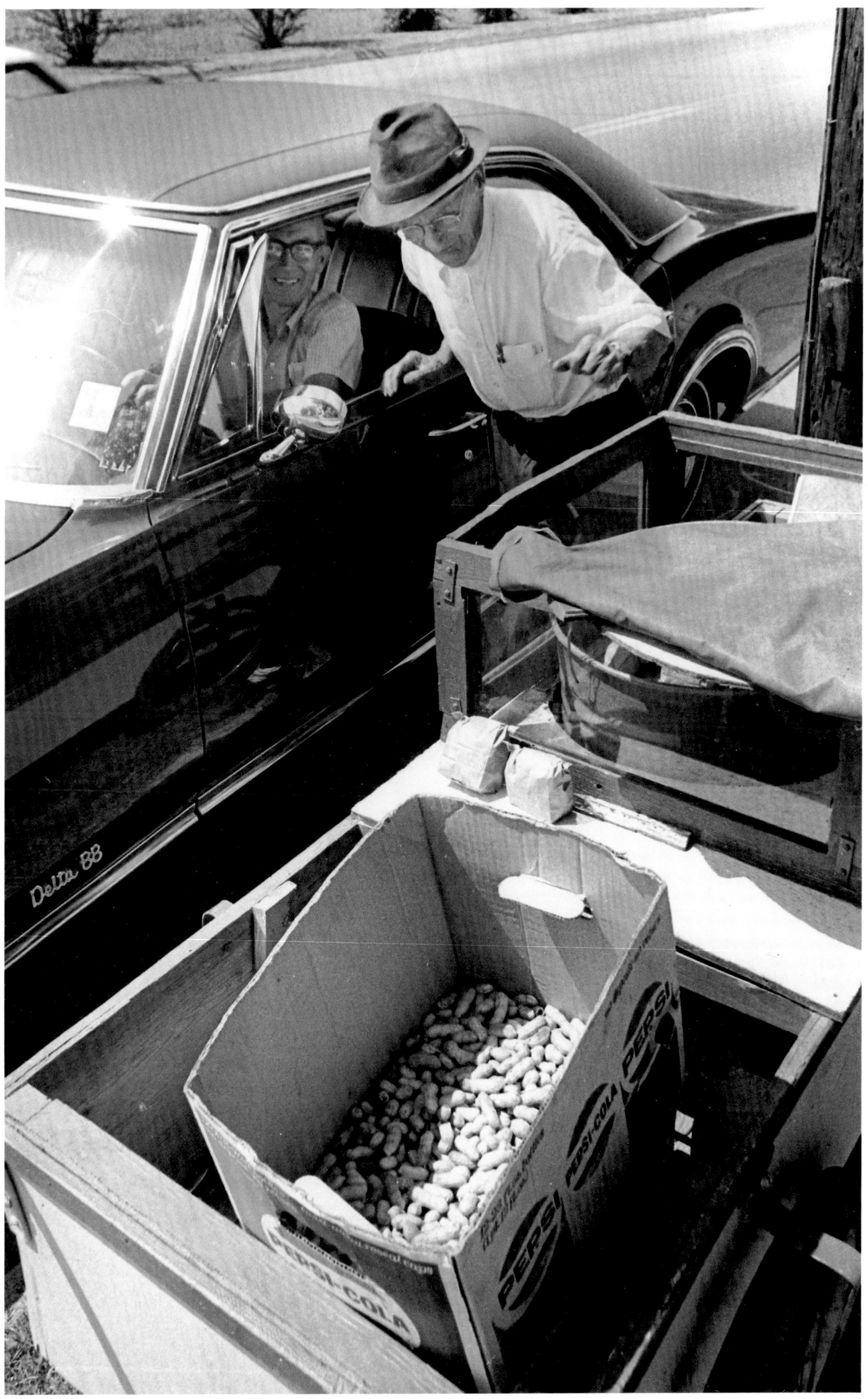

Delta 88
PEPSI-COLA

They said, 'Sam, you'll never roast peanuts on that,' but I have.

"Put the peanuts in the winder and I just sit there and turn that crank so they get done right. Folks say, 'Sam, that'll take a long time.' It does. Takes an hour. But I got nothin' else better to do."

During lulls in the conversation and between peanut sales, Sam liked to read. Under the tree lay the remains of a newspaper, and a book titled *Life Begins at Death*. Sam said he liked books, especially poetry. And with that, the old peanutman stood up and began reciting:

> Under the spreading chestnut tree
> The village smithy stands
> The smith, a mighty man is he
> With large and sinewy hands
> And the muscles of his brawny arms
> Are strong as iron bands . . .

Sam pulled back his sleeve and flexed his right arm in a little knot to illustrate the recitation, and he smiled at his performance. Perhaps "Handy" Haynes liked to envision himself as independent and self-reliant as Longfellow's heroic figure, a valued and vital part of the community. He may have only been a peanutman, but he was proud just the same.

A large, black car pulled up before the peanut stand. Again, Sam rocketed off his pail and did his bent little dance routine over to the car's window. "Haynes, I been missin' you!" the driver called out.

"My wife's been sick," Sam responded apologetically. "You like them peanuts I sold you pretty well?" he asked hopefully.

"Yes indeed," the customer responded, buying two bags and insisting that Sam take a whole quarter for the pair. When the big spender drove off, Sam stared at the quarter in his hand. "He tipped me a nickel," he said happily. "Think he must be a big man over at the mill."

Sam returned to his shady spot under the tree where he resumed the comfortable conversation with Guffey the appleman. Silhouetted against the glaring June sun and the Main Street traffic, the two old vendors looked like a montage from another age superimposed over a twentieth-century setting.

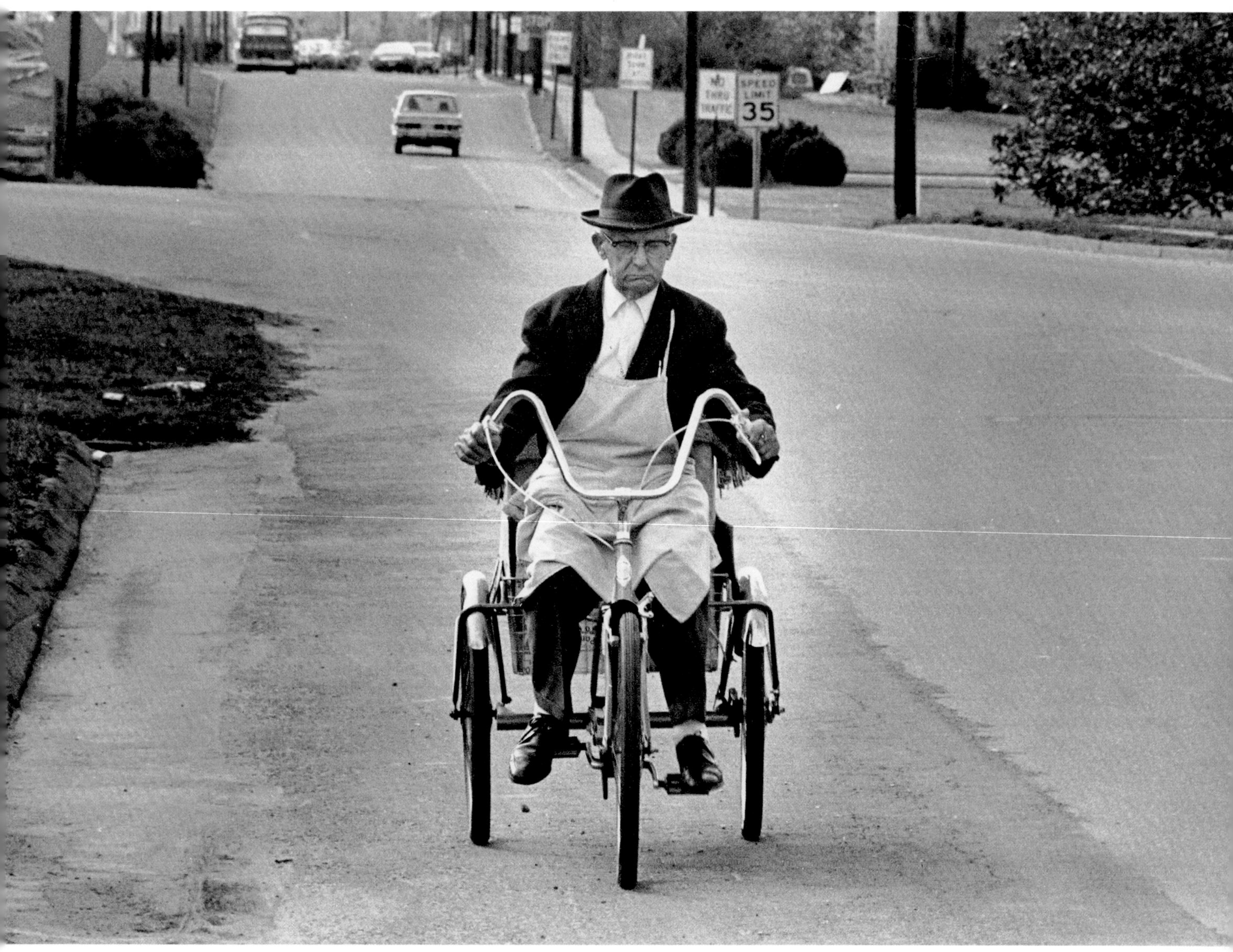

"Handy" uses a tricycle for his peanut deliveries.

Edsel Martin, Woodcarver

I'm the laziest man in the county . . .

The natural good humor of Edsel Martin flowed down his arms, through his fingers, past the keen blade of his carving knife, and into the basswood figures. Wood chips, like individual peals of silent laughter, fell about his feet.

Scholars called him a folk artist. But Edsel, in his endearing, self-effacing way proclaimed himself instead "the laziest man in the county." That was his real claim to fame, he insisted. His wood-carving he disparaged as "drib-drabbing around."

But Edsel's drib-drabbing was displayed in prestigious craft shops from Asheville to the Smithsonian Institution. His work, particularly his figurines, had a sense of humor about them—the very same airy, understated humor of their maker.

It was a long way from the Smithsonian to Edsel's place. With his wife Elsie, he lived with a near-blind old poodle named Curly and a cat that was fond of being stroked and biting back. The driveway leading to Edsel's house crept on all fours through a cavernous, laurel-choked cove near Old Fort. It was remote—and Edsel liked it that way.

He was a big, solid man with a generous mustache, and eyes that seemed to be dancing elusively like the sun behind passing clouds. He gave the impression at first of being uninterested, but then those dancing eyes would give him away. He never said his

Master craftsman Edsel Martin of Old Fort
at work on a dulcimer;
he calls it "drib-drabbing."

"

age, nor did it matter; he was a merry, ageless wood spirit with magical hands: a block of wood became a mountain warbler, a cardinal with a cocked head, a dulcimer with a sad-eyed hound dog or plaintive-faced mountain girl on the instrument's scroll.

"It just come in my family," Edsel said, characteristically modest. "What I know I contribute to them. My father was a fiddlemaker. He was the one started carving heads on the scrolls of fiddles. Carved a lion's head on a fiddle once." Cradling a cup of coffee, Edsel leaned against a table on an open side porch where he liked to work. A dulcimer scroll was taking shape nearby—this one with a hound dog head carved in a permanent snarl staring down the length of the stringboard. "Ain't he ugly?" Edsel said approvingly.

Falling silent, Edsel appeared to be pondering something. Then he sighed in resignation like a backwoods Jack Benny delivering his dry punchline, "I could really get some work done if I'd work steady like I ought to. But I gotta run the roads a lot. Run the roads . . . gotta go someplace and loaf around."

After all, there was his reputation to think about. A puppeteer over in Greenlee, Clyde Hollifield, was crowding Edsel for the title of The Laziest Man. "I can't let Clyde get into first place," vowed the big man with the barest trace of a wink.

State Fair officials had invited Edsel to participate in the "living folk demonstration" at the fair that year, but he wasn't so sure if he wanted to go; that sounded a lot like work to him. He had worked for three years steady at the Highlands Crafts Guild shop outside Asheville. "Crafts got to be pretty lively back in the sixties when dulcimers got big—I didn't make anything but dulcimers. But I've grown tired of 'em. I keep on making one now and again so I don't forget how."

Edsel had also tried his hand at music-making. "Played a liddlebidda this and a liddlebidda that. Fretless banjo with Billy Ed Wheeler—you know, he wrote 'Coward of the County,' 'Jackson,' 'Little Brown Shack,' 'Long Arm of the Law,' and 'The Reverend Mr. Black.'"

Another dramatic stage sigh. "Now he's rich—and here I sit . . . in this old dump . . ."

But the music-making and crafts scene had changed drastically by the eighties, he said. "There's a lotta people doing crafts nowadays who used to didn't do it," alluding to Appalachian dulcimer kits from Taiwan. "Most people who come here to get my dulcimers already have one or two."

Edsel had also made about five guitars. "They weren't half-bad, but they take too much work." So he turned to carving figures because "you know, I'm always looking for the easiest way out."

Elsie, who had just walked in with a bunch of flowers she'd carved from maple sprigs, apologized helplessly, "He's the greatest kidder."

Edsel went right on as if he hadn't heard Elsie's aside. Holding up a wooden cardinal with its head twisted inquisitively to one side, he knit his brows in consternation. "You know, it's really hard to get their heads to turn like that. You have to soak 'em overnight and then twist the wood in a vise . . ." Elsie rolled her eyes heavenward, and made sure Edsel added that Jim Hunt, the former governor of North Carolina, had purchased a dozen of Edsel's cardinals to give as Christmas presents.

Then it was out the workshop door, where a lifesize wooden maiden in the nude had been known to startle unprepared visitors. Passing the voluptuous figure, Edsel just smiled inwardly, giving her a pat. Elsie pretended not to notice.

Edsel led the way to the trailer he used to take to craft shows. There, he showed off one of his favorite carvings that he kept under a bell jar: an old granny woman bent over a scrub board, a flop-eared hound asleep at her feet. "I do like to do my figures best of all. I just do ol' mountain people."

The carving had caught the attention of the Smithsonian. A letter from its director implored Edsel to attend the annual Festival of American Folklife. "No such exhibition would be complete without one of your carvings and a dulcimer," the director had written. That letter seemed to satisfy Edsel more than money.

Shutting the parked trailer, Edsel wound his way up past the garden to a weatherboarded barn where he kept his main workshop.

Sitting in a cane-bottomed chair he went to trimming a woman's head on the scroll of a dulcimer. Wood chips rained down his pants leg to add to the sweet carpeting of slivers and sawdust.

"I just use a regular ol' pocketknife to carve with—and a liddlebiddy carving knife for little places," he offered, as if to say: anybody could do what I do, and probably better.

A Martin masterpiece bound for the Smithsonian Institution.

It was cool there in the semi-dark of the workshop barn. The June morning light fell gently through the open door, silhouetting the man quietly at work. In the next stall a rooster and chickens gawked and chatted comfortably amongst themselves. A basket over the workbench revealed half a dozen wood-dusty eggs. They could have been carved or laid; it was difficult to tell. On the workbench a wooden covey of hummingbirds, wrens, mockers, and cardinals lay flocked about awaiting Edsel's return.

Elsie appeared at the door, shadowed by her three-year-old granddaughter. Taking the shy, lovely girl in her lap, Elsie chatted easily with the woodcarver at work. The talk was pleasant and soft—as friendly as the nearby brook that chuckled its way past Edsel Martin's workshop.

Part Two **The Land**

This land, no matter how rocky, it'll still grow fine Christmas trees. And I'm happy my kids—and now these grandboys will be comin' along—and I hope growin' trees on this same land when I'm gone. That's why I'm gonna hang onto this land if I can. Folks say, "Shoot, Joe. You oughta sell that land for condominiums and make a bundle." But hello! I'll not do it.

—Joe Henson

Aunt Kate Burnette, Woodcutting Farmwoman

I'm just as old-timey as I can be.

"**A**in't nobody as homey as me." Aunt Kate Burnette's double-bladed ax slapped into the beech log. "Mister, I'm just what I am—and I don't care. I'm just an ol' wood-gatherer."

"Thwack!" went Aunt Kate's ax, imbedded in the end of the log as she bludgeoned the thing in two by repeated beatings on a weathered chopping block.

"I'm just as old-timey as I can be. Soon be eighty-seven. And I do love to chop wood and saw. Always done it. Had to, y'know." The old woman peered cheerfully through her glasses, shaded by a green translucent eyeshade, which allowed her white hair to go unfettered.

She wore a short-sleeved dress with long sleeves of a different pattern sewed on to protect her arms. Sturdy shoes and an apron held up by safety pins completed her practical woodcutter's outfit. Seated in an ancient, once-red chair ("almost as old as me!") Aunt Kate was the reigning matriarch of Mackey's Creek in McDowell County.

Aunt Kate's secure world was centered on her little house with its treasured "Mazoo" wood cookstove; a flower garden ringing the

"And I do love to chop wood and saw," exclaims
eighty-six-year-old Aunt Kate Burnette of Mackey's Creek.

place with coreopsis, zinnias, and scarlet sage; a vegetable garden gone to gangly "mole beans" and morning glories; a silver-gray woodshed "me 'n' Poor Ol' Dad built"; and a hose draped over a steering wheel mounted on a pole that created a little creek in her front yard from the constancy of the gravity-fed water.

Aunt Kate liked to sit outside in the cool shade of the woodshed, surrounded by the ten-foot-tall ramparts of fresh-sawed beech stove wood, and recollect early times when she and her late, much-beloved husband Gordon (whom she called "Poor Ol' Dad") "couldn't scrape up ten cents between us."

She began: "I was borned over on Crooked Creek where Papa had a li'l dab o' land. He died when I was three years old. My mother, poor ol' thing, there never was a better mother, she raised the three of us. We sure did have a hard go of it. That's where I learned to gather wood.

"I didn't get to the fourth grade. Went to a free school over at Ebeneezer. Walked about three to five miles. Sometimes we wouldn't go when it was too cold—for we didn't have warm enough clothes. When we did go, they had a great big ol' chimney for to keep a good fire in the school. They'd let school out for fodder-pullin' time. Well, I never did get educated. An' I never did amount to nothin', mister!" Aunt Kate laughed at her own joke with great enjoyment. "Back then school wasn't required. To think about that—back then we didn't know no better."

She married Gordon Burnette in 1910. "He farmed all his life. Or worked in the sand pit. Never did have a public job. Wouldn't take WPA. We cut chestnut logs together and hauled 'em by mule and wagon to the tannery in Old Fort. The roads was so bad, why, sometimes we'd be stuck so's we'd have to climb the poaches to get the mules going again." She described the spokes—"poaches"— of the wagon wheels with her outstretched fingers.

"We had three children. We lost one little boy when he was four years old," she said sadly. Then brightening, she resumed, "At first, we lived in a two-room shack. I'll tell you what, it was built outa green lumber and it shrunk. We took newspapers and I crammed the cracks to keep the weather out. But I can still remember when I had our first baby, it commenced a-snowin' the last week of Oc-tober and it stayed till spring back in those big ol' coves on the north side of the hill. I remember it blowed snow on the quilt and

Aunt Kate displays a picture she took of her late husband, "Poor Ol' Dad," surrounded by their children.

Poor Ol' Dad'd have to shake the quilt coverin' me 'n' the baby."

Aunt Kate reflected, "Every generation, why—it seems like they got up a step higher. But we lived simple and we was happy. We had our own chickens, hogs, and a cow. About all we had to buy was salt, or coffee. Why, I tell you it was rough at times but we just had a happy life.

"We picked galax and sprays of dog-hobble way back up in the mountains. Had to walk six or seven miles back up there. That's hard work—galax pickin'. But I always thought the best eatin' was the lunches we'd take galax pickin'. It'd be so cold way off up there. And we'd set down with some ham meat, and some biscuits I'd make that morning, and an erngun. . . . What's that? *Erngun?* Oh, that's what we used to call onions. Didn't nobody say onion then. Called 'em ernguns." Aunt Kate enunciated precisely like a school marm.

"Other times we'd take ol' Mike the ox and a sled with high standards, and we'd go up on the mountain and cut a load of chestnut wood with a crosscut saw. Now back then, they didn't know no such thing as a chain saw.

"Used to plow with ol' Mike. Just the garden plot by myself. But one day Dad said, 'Mammy, you move that pile o' brash.' But just about the time I had it loaded, that ol' bull took a notion he'd run away. And he took off yon side of the bluff. Ol' Uncle Dan Walker was out a-plowin' and that bull come a-chargin' down through there. Scared him so's he was a-hollerin', 'Orta be against the law to let a bull run loose in the road.'

"That ol' bull run plumb down the road with me a-chasin' him barefoot. I didn't wear no shoes back then. Didn't need 'em, for my feet was tough."

The sun was moving toward the woodshed by now, and Aunt Kate elected to move her chair into the bright October sunlight. With a small friendly dog named Sammie-Joe at her feet, Aunt Kate remembered the time she scared the daylights out of Poor Ol' Dad's mule, Frank.

Her husband had asked her to water the mule, and "outa pure meanness, I just let 'im have it right in the face with the water bucket. Why, I tell you, mister, it scared that ol' mule sick. He 'bout tore down the stable—and he carried on and cried all day. And every time Poor Ol' Dad went to water that mule—when

Frank saw that bucket, he went mad. I didn't tell Dad for a month what I'd done."

Then there was the time good cooking saved her life. "Used to be there wasn't but four houses between here and the highway—and there was tramps, I guess you'd call 'em, who'd come by kind of regular. They'd ask for something to eat and I'd always give 'em something. Well, one day this man came up and he was carrying two grips—satchels, you'd call 'em. He asked for something to eat, and I fixed him some ham meat." Aunt Kate paused, and then went on, "He'd left his satchels on the porch. But the sow'd had a litter of baby pigs—ten or more—and the porch was low and the little pigs used to come up there just like the dogs, so I carried the satchels in the front room for fear that the little pigs come and bother them. Well, I noticed how heavy they was. 'My Lord,' I thought to myself, 'What's in here?'

"Well, we got to talking, and the man went to asking me about who was the postmaster at Old Fort, and who was the postmaster at Black Mountain, and such like that—and directly I mentioned that I'd moved his grips inside. You know what? He yanked his chair back and jumped up and hollered, 'You done WHAT to my satchels? Why'd you touch those things?!' And I knew for sure he's a burglar. Well, I had a feeling he's gonna kill me then and there, but he calmed down when he saw his satchels was all right, and he said, 'Lady, I'll tell you, anybody that treats me as nice and cooks for me as good as you have—I'll never harm.'

"Well, he went on, and directly Dad came home and you can bet neither one of us slept that night for fear that he'd return and kill us both. And then not long after that we heard that the post office in Old Fort and Black Mountain had been robbed—and then there was *his* picture in the paper!" Aunt Kate finished with a flourish, "How'dja like that? I gave dinner to a burglar."

Aunt Kate pondered, "Don't have tramps no more. Used to be there'd be people that just wandered for their livin'. Now, you can't trust people like you used to could.

"Two men got out of a truck recently and come up on me. Well, mister, I just picked up a big ol' stick and waited. They just wanted directions or something. But if I'd a-had to, I coulda used that stick. Yessir!"

Kate's son Paul dropped by for a visit and wanted to tell about the time the fearless old woman "almost shot that man with the wooden .45."

"Oh, Lordy," Aunt Kate shook her head in dismay.

Paul began the story: "I was off making music, and I'd left my ol' hound dog that'd bite at home here with Aunt Kate. That night a distant relative stopped by to see Kate for some reason, and the man came up on the porch past the dog and knocked on the door. Kate hollered out, 'Who's there?' and the man didn't answer. She called out again and again no answer."

At this point in the story, Aunt Kate took over the telling. "I had that old pokin' stick from the fire, but that wouldn't do. Then I spied that old gun—a wooden .45 pistol that Paul had whittled out of a board. I grabbed that pistol off the wall, and jerked open the front door. The full moon was a-shinin' and I plugged that wooden gun in the poor man's stomach.

"'If you move, I'll shoot your heart out!' I remember saying. And it scared 'im so bad, he fell back'ards off the porch, cross't that ol' hound dog, knocked two chairs over, and fell down into the front yard—jumped up and took off runnin' . . ." Aunt Kate couldn't hide her embarrassment. "Y'know, I was sick in bed for two weeks after that—for I know if that'd been a real gun I woulda shot him. That scared me so."

Aunt Kate earned her affectionate title "Aunt" when she worked for the Mackeys down the road, the family that had owned much of the valley. The children she tended were calling her "Mrs. Burnette" until Mrs. Mackey asked if they might not call her Aunt Kate. She assented and the name stuck.

"People just got hung up on calling me Aunt Kate. I even get mailed addressed like that."

Always a hard-working country woman, Aunt Kate used to take in washing, scrubbed on her homemade washboard down by the creek. "People'd call me a washerwoman—but I didn't care. I used to work for fifty cents a day. Lord, I said, if I could earn a dollar a day, how my prayers would be answered. Then, when I was fifty-three years old I went to work in the furniture factory and earned forty cents an hour! I knowed I was rich then. Imagine that—after earning fifty cents a *day*.

"We used to wake up at four in the morning. Poor Ol' Dad'd start the wood cookstove, and then I'd get up, make biscuits, eggs, and cereal. Then I'd light my lantern and go milk the two cows, strain my milk—and that for my sister—wash my dishes, and walk to the highway to meet my work bus. By then it'd be about six o'clock in the morning. Now, that's how I got along. Didn't make no difference if it's snowing or raining—I'se there just the same."

Aunt Kate wondered at the changes. "Now people can just step outa their door, get in their car, and drive to work. Unh-*huhnn*! My daughter does that."

When she retired, Aunt Kate went to file for Social Security— and when asked if she'd supported her husband the last year, she replied truthfully, "Not entirely, for last year Dad sold a thousand-dollar option on some gravel." So the official told her, "I guess you know that knocks you out of half of what you'd get otherwise."

Aunt Kate continued, "When the word got around Mackey's Creek what I'd done, some of 'em back here teased me for telling 'em that. But I'da been condemned every time I'd go to the mailbox to get my check. Well, I would! I'd be thinking to myself, 'Well Lord, I lied.'"

After her husband's death, Aunt Kate kept on fending for herself with the same sort of independence that had marked her life. Her garden was an annual marvel. A typical Mackey's Creek sight in summer was Aunt Kate sitting in that old red chair hoeing her vegetable patch. Her full freezer on the front porch always testified to her green thumb.

But a couple years back, that freezer got her in trouble. Cleaning out some newspapers that had fallen behind the freezer, "I felt something hit me on the leg," she recalled. "I looked down—and Lord, there was a copperhead. It was only about fourteen inches long but it hit me just the same. They tease me that I went out in the road and called out, '*Whoo! Snake Bite! Whoo! Snake Bite!*'

"They come and got me and as we're going to the hospital, my son Paul, poor thing, kept on asking me, 'Mammy, are you sick? Mammy, do you feel sick?'

"And I said, 'Son, listen: we don't know what's gonna happen. But if something *is* gonna happen to me, I just want you to know your mama didn't have to wait to get snakebit to get ready to die— 'cause I'm already ready.'

"But I come through it. Felt nauseated only once't, though. My leg swole up blue for two weeks," she said.

It was getting on to dinner time, and Aunt Kate stirred from her chair. "Can't look up or get up too fast. Got inner-ear. Makes me dizzy-like," she apologized. "But the good Lord has been good to me. I thank Him for my good health."

Walking across the sun-splashed yard, beneath the chestnut tree blooming for a second time that fall, past the gurgling fountain of spring water by the roadside, Aunt Kate gazed off across the meadow where Hub Myer's black angus cattle wearing bells on their collars ding-donkled distantly.

Aunt Kate stopped beside a giant beech tree, its limbs recently cut back for improved health and cookstove fuel. "Poor Ol' Dad set that beech tree out," Aunt Kate said softly, as if to herself. Perhaps she was envisioning a man in overalls down on his knees toiling with a sapling in the soil. "Well, mister," Aunt Kate said matter-of-factly, "I'm gonna go in and eat me some ernguns and beans now. Got me some apples drying on the stove. And the good Lord bless you, too."

Sammie-Joe watches closely
as Aunt Kate Burnette
splits another beech log.

Silhouetted with his Christmas trees,
Avery County grower Joe Henson prunes each tree.
"You get him a-shapin' up towards the sky, yeah boy . . ."

Joe Henson, Christmas-Tree Grower

I'm doin' what I love to do. I swear, I enjoy it.

Joe Henson, sixty, eased the battered pickup truck into four-wheel drive and sent the vehicle jouncing like a carnival bump-car up the treacherous incline toward the shrubbery patch. The veteran grower shouted over the engine's roar: "I really enjoy life. And it's a good living. But everything we've got, we came by the hard way. I've done every dang thing to make a living—dug ditches, put up hay, dug shrubbery on the mountain. . . . But now the kids are grown and educated and doin' well. We just flew in and built us a house—and now it feels pretty good."

Joe, an irrepressible bear of a man, had made his own way in the world by growing and selling shrubbery from Crossnore, where his home county of Avery proudly declared itself the "Shrubbery Capital of the World." What really helped Joe turn the corner was the growing of fraser firs for Christmas trees.

At Joe's upland nurseries, tucked between Soapstone Mountain, the Potato Hill, and Hawshaw Mountain, he and his family tended about eight thousand trees of which he sold roughly eight hundred a year.

"It's just a gamble though," he said, pulling a soiled "Bull Rider" billed cap down over a ruggedly handsome face. "It's nine years before I'm gonna realize anything out of these new seedlings."

As the seed beds and Christmas-tree hills came into view, Joe recounted the litany of patience and nurturing required of the Christmas-tree grower. "Been doin' it for twenty-two years. First seedlings come off The Roan. Then the state nurseries started selling 'em. At first the state they begged folks to buy 'em. They were sixty-five dollars a thousand. Now, it's one hundred dollars a thousand. It's a lot higher but they're easier to get.

"The state beds the seedlings for three years. The grower buys 'em and they're called 'three-O's.' You've got to bed 'em for another two years. So it's five years before they're ready to transplant to the field. Well, you've got to have your land prepared. You line your place off; each tree goes in four feet apart. You get twenty-seven hundred trees per acre. Then there's weedkiller to put down, fertilizer in the spring; you got to shape 'em up and spray or treat for red spider or balsam woolly aphid, mow between 'em. . . . It takes five to seven years to make a six-to-seven-foot-tall tree that I'll get twelve to fifteen dollars for.

"The buyer generally comes up here and picks, cuts, bales, and hauls the trees to a lot which he's got to rent. It ain't no wonder they're goin' for twenty-five dollars," Joe said, stopping the pickup and stepping out to survey the fields.

This he did with obvious satisfaction. Before him spread the rank and file of his labors: shiny steeples in columns neatly marching across the meadow for a hundred yards. Beyond the green regiments Grandfather Mountain loomed against a balmy November sky.

Joe, a man in his element, strode easily through the rows, knowledgeably pruning here and there with a pocketknife, which he used as deftly as an extra set of fingers—always shaping the trees as they seemed to need it—while he cussed the occasional aphid damage. "Dang li'l mites," he growled.

"The idea is to get this tree goin' like an upside-down ice cream cone," Joe advised. "You get him a-shapin' up toward the sky, yeah boy . . ." Joe stood back to admire a particularly nice tree: "Now, ain't he a dandy?"

Not all trees are so perfectly shaped. Those that Joe called "kinda cully" had another chance. Always speaking of the tree in the third person masculine, Joe lectured, "By shapin' him up and givin' him another year, I can make him fill out." Trees that are hopeless culls can still be profitable when branches are sold for wreaths, roping, and sprays.

Some growers prefer to have their trees with root systems balled in burlap so the trees will stay fresh longer—and that also makes it possible to plant them after Christmas. But Joe cautioned, "There ain't a bit of use to set out a balled fraser fir in the flatlands like down in Charlotte or Raleigh, 'cause he just won't do. It's too warm. Marion's about the limit off the mountain.

Once a balled tree is dug or cut, the hole must be filled or a new seedling has to be planted to replace the old one. While the little five-year-old tree grows, the stump rots. Looking across Joe Henson's Christmas-tree hills, one could see various stages of phoenix-like growth in progress all around.

The balsam woolly aphid, which has given foresters such a problem in wild stands of Appalachian evergreens, was fairly easy to control in the Christmas-tree fields. Joe said he sprinkled a tablespoon of peppery-looking insecticide at the base of the trees every year. The poison worked through the root system and spread upward to kill the aphid. Still, in places the little insect had stunted some of Joe's trees. Scratching his head, Joe wondered aloud, "I'm bumfuzzled why some trees react differently to the danged mite than others."

Joe climbed to the top of one of his Christmas-tree hills where he had a favorite picnic spot. A weathered oak table supported his considerable but solid bulk. Joe nodded toward Grandfather Mountain: "Ol' Gran'pappy. That's some view, ain't it?"

Across the hills and coves, the chimes of the Baptist church down in Crossnore—two miles away—echoed faintly like a distant music box. Joe avowed reflectively, "I'm doin' what I love to do. I swear, I enjoy it.

"This land, no matter how rocky, it'll still grow fine Christmas trees. And I'm happy my kids—and now these grandboys will be comin' along—and I hope growin' trees on this same land when I'm gone. That's why I'm gonna hang onto this land if I can. Folks say, 'Shoot, Joe. You oughta sell that land for condominiums and make a bundle.' But hello! I'll not do it."

Even though his livelihood depended on Christmas, Joe was not jaded to the joys of the season. "Hot dang!" he grinned. "But when we go to cuttin' and diggin' and you get that stuff—the fraser fir sap and resin—on your hands . . . why, it smells like Christmas!"

Joe was toying with the idea of selling small, inexpensive balled trees for "people who live in trailers and don't have room for a big tree. Folks who want a real tree but who can't put out twenty-five dollars for one."

He added: "Wouldn't it be a good idea if I got into some sort of cut-your-own-Christmas-tree deal? A man could bring his family up here, pick out their tree for maybe fifteen dollars, and then let one of the young'uns take a little bow saw and cut their own Christmas tree. . . . Don't you know they'd never forget it? I'd like to develop that idea. It might be more trouble for you to drive up from say, Marion, but then you'd be doin' it for the experience— y'know what I mean?"

Back at the house, Emmaline Henson had prepared a pre-Thanksgiving feast for the grower "home from the hill."

"These farm boys like to eat at dinner time," Emmaline explained, loading the table with fried chicken, their own home-grown beans, corn, and potatoes, as well as her locally celebrated biscuits and gravy; and daughter Martha Jo's slaw—plus fried apples and raspberry-and-strawberry shortcake.

Joe took the occasion to describe early days in the shrubbery business after World War Two when he and partner Sam Cuthbertson "used to go over on Brown Mountain and live from Monday to Friday in a danged shack. Dug punktatum and red laurel and one thing and the other. Dug on that mountain for so long. But it was the life," he said with a smile.

Emmaline just shook her head, looking at Joe. "When he dies, it'll be the last of a breed," she teased affectionately.

But Joe had no intention of that ever happening. At the table when little four-year-old "grandboy" Jeremy had seriously asked his "Paw-Paw" how the Christmas trees grew and reproduced, Joe Henson had taken delight in patiently explaining the process, and the little mountain boy hadn't missed a word.

Joe envelops a granddaughter
with one of his bear-hugs.

WILD
RIDER

Ninety-six-year-old Laura Presnell
recalls old farming days along the headwaters of the Catawba:
"I was stout as a mule, sure enough."

Laura Presnell, Farmwoman

Yeah boy, I'd rather plow as to hoe . . .

She was frail, but her smiling eyes so dominated a face full of tracery lines that she emanated an air of strength. Laura Allison Presnell had been a tough farmwoman back up at the headwaters of the Catawba above Old Fort. At ninety-six, she had lost neither her steely core nor her memory.

"I was stout as a mule, sure enough. Why, I plowed many a day and what I'm a-talkin' about you don't hardly see no men plowin' nowadays. Yeah boy, I'd rather plow as to hoe. Hoein' was hard work. And I did hoe when I had to. Cooked, scrubbed clothes on the washboard down by the river. How'd I steer that mule, y'say? Why, I'd say, 'Gee' for left, and 'Whoa-*haw!*' for right," Laura threw her head back and laughed at the sound of the old command.

"Times have changed, sure have. Used to drink water right out of the river. Had no electricity at first. We never owned a car. Cooked on the woodstove or in the fireplace. Had a horse and wagon, but I've walked the five miles to Sunday school many a times down to Old Fort. We'd go every Sunday if the weather was fit. Had to cross the river two or three times by footlog. If it was getting high, then we'd turn around and go back. What made that kind of living bearable was that neighbors helped each other. Corn shuckin's, quiltin's, helpin' each other get the crop in. Folks don't do that anymore. Well, it's just pure laziness, that's it. Back then people helped each other. Now they don't.

"I can remember the hard times too, buddy. And yet . . . y'know that was a happy life back then. Yeah, it was hard then—but now in a way I think it's harder."

She was born in 1885 to Ken and Nancy Allison whose farm bordered the left fork of the headwaters of the Catawba. "Daddy was a farmer, but when he'd go off to work for fifty cents a day, why, Mother she'd keep the farm. Mommy helped him side by side. She learned me to cook on the open fireplace and to quilt. I been quiltin' ever since I was a liddlebiddy thing. And buddy, I better sew it right too, or Mother'd make me rip it out a dozen times, but I kept my mouth shut," she said with a grin.

"Dad he'd get up at four o'clock in the morning and get the fire goin'. Then he'd set there a-straddle that chair and sing till Mommy'd get up. Yeah boy, 'How Firm a Foundation,' that's one I'll never forget. And my daddy could sing, too."

"I got to studying about it—and I can't get it fixed how our parents raised us. If we had to work that hard now . . ."

Laura attended a one-room, ungraded school typical of the region and times, with students from first-graders on up all in the same room. "It was just one room, is what I'm laughing about," she said, grinning. "It had a wood heater right in the middle, and our parents would furnish the wood. Yeah, we stayed good and warm. It was a free school, and I went through the ninth grade."

Laura married James Presnell "after we's sweethearts for twelve years. I told him, 'It's marry or quit for good,'" she said, beaming. They built a house near her parents' place, and the couple started farming. The Presnells had no children, so Laura could devote her energies to being James's farming partner. "We raised everything but our sugar, flour and coffee," she said affirmatively. "That was all we had to go to the store for. We had two milk cows, and I milked two times a day. Churned and sold my milk and butter to neighbors around. Had chickens and hogs, so we had our own meat. Kept bees for honey. And raised molasses. Kate the mule pulled the molasses mill. Lord, no, folks wouldn't know what to do today if they had to manage like we did.

"I never did own an electric stove. It was wood or nothin'. We'd have fried chicken or ham, beans, taters, cornbread and biscuits, fresh milk and butter—yeah boy! On that ol' wood stove. And didn't my kitchen smell good!"

The Presnells had to generate their own entertainment, so they relied on church and neighbors to provide social occasions. "We went to church a lot. And people'd come plumb from Black Mountain to visit. They'd stay to get their dinner, and why yes, sometimes they'd stay the night. People'd come sometimes to squirrel hunt, and we kept guns—and boy, I could use it. There was bear and deer in the cornfields."

After James's death in 1956, Laura stayed at Lake James Rest Home. Then she moved to a rest home in Forest City, but she was spending this fall in Goose Creek, McDowell County, where her first cousin Rena Elliott had urged her to come stay for a spell. Laura insisted on earning her keep by babysitting and piecing and sewing quilt tops. "Might near everybody in the family's got one now," she said of her quilts. "And I made one for my doctor and, boy, he was delighted to have him one. But right after that he told me he wanted me to quit on account of my health. Well, I told him, 'Now you've got yours and you want me to quit!'" she said with a laugh.

Laura wasn't surprised that even city folks were starting to see the worth of old quilts, plain living, and family history. "They've come plumb from Salisbury worryin' me about the Allison family history, askin' me questions till I was wore tee-totally out!" she complained happily. She really didn't mind at all. "People will have to come back to the old way yet. Looks like they'll have to."

Harold M. Clark, Nurseryman

Something is radically screwball!

Harold M. Clark, seventy, was a Johnny-Appleseed-Come-Lately. Except in this old nurseryman's case, his passion wasn't broadcasting apple trees—but rather, the California laurel.

In 1965 Harold concluded, after tending his nursery in Oregon, that the California laurel could grow best in the southern Appalachians where its cousin, the mountain laurel, grew wild. He had spent the better part of his life trying to get the laurel to take hold in northern and western nurseries, but with little success. He wanted people to accept the laurel for what he thought it was: the fastest growing high-quality hardwood known.

Harold's amazing hardwood would replace the relatively low-quality but fast-growing Southern pines and revolutionize the building industry. This was the old man's dream.

But Harold knew he was getting old. Time was growing short for him to prove to the world that he held the secret of the wonder tree; this called for a bold move.

So he took his rusted 1958 Chevrolet (which looked as if Rommel had used it in his Sahara campaign), stripped the car's seats out—with the exception of the driver's place, and carefully crammed the car with thirty thousand seedlings and three hundred plants until there was just enough room for Clark's Falstaffian figure to wedge behind the wheel.

"Cheesusgawd, if people think I'm some sort of hippie—well, let 'em think what they want," explodes nurseryman Harold Clark.

After consulting weather, soil, and climatic maps and charts, Harold chose his destination: a perfect site for the growing of his rolling nursery, in a thermal belt identical to that of the laurel's West Coast habitat—just east of the Blue Ridge in Rutherford County. It was a place called Sandy Mush.

The dilapidated Chevy couldn't have held another seedling. All but engulfed in his traveling arboretum, Harold had set out across America—a trek of three thousand miles. Like Johnny Appleseed before him, the old nurseryman's needs were simple. But not so with his steed. The car, groaning with the weight of its green burden, broke down so many times in the crossing that by the time Harold drove it into Sandy Mush he had only fifteen cents left. The unsinkable Irish Bostonian chortled grimly, "Goddamitey! That's what I call cutting it close!"

He settled in a simple, unheated, uninsulated frame farmhouse that offered few creature comforts. All that mattered to him was the soil and the climate, and the growing of his precious laurel trees.

Looking back on his frustrating saga, Harold was bitter. But an ironic sense of humor kept him laughing at the rough hand he felt fate had dealt him. "Cheesusgawd," he bellowed at the thought of the misinformation supplied him by university-trained horticulturists. "Something is radically screwball!" he practically shouted, shaking a ruddy mane and an ample, gray-streaked beard. "I says to myself—you can't tell a college professor nothing. It tickles me: ha, ha, ha!" he laughed like a dog barking.

Sitting in front of his makeshift worktable in the midst of his backyard nursery, Harold reviewed his pilgrim's progress while potting fresh cuttings. Perspiration stained a faded, short-sleeved sweatshirt and once-green suspenders attached to black, knee-length shorts. Dark socks and desert boots completed the practical ensemble.

Harold laughed bitterly about his encounters with experts at Yale, Rutgers, Maryland, and Harvard. "Harvard!" he snorted. "They don't even know about the tree at Harvard. Lookit this," he said, brandishing one letter in which a professor responded, 'I have found evidence that the seed might germinate . . .'"

Harold exploded, "Might germinate! Cheesusgoddamitey. He's a beauty! A scientific marvel, that one. Ha, ha, ha. . . . You can't

tell 'em anything. Sheesh, whattaya gonna do with these guys? I tell 'em, but nobody'll come down here and see this. Look at my trees growing. What more proof do you need?" he glared at this year's crop.

It took him four years to get a crop to take hold. Harold thought he had found the secret. His little forest of hardwood evergreens were charging out of the ground—eight inches in their first year. Harold was ecstatic. "I came here partly because of the longer growing season. I've learned something every year—and this year is the first time I've done well. Y'see I tried to get the college brains to figure out how to grow 'em in the East. Holycheesus, but I've been through a lot: lost the plants once in a New York freeze, another time I gave twenty thousand seeds to an arboretum in Delaware but only a dozen survived."

The sweat plastered his salt and pepper hair to his tanned forehead as he talked and worked. "It's a dual-purpose tree," he said. "Also called the bay laurel. The leaves are used in cooking. A French cook'd throw away his pots and pans without the bay leaf. There's recipes by the million that calls for the bay leaf. You gotta have it."

Harold continued potting the fresh cuttings according to his special method: he gently wedged the cutting into a mixture of fertilizer, soil, and plant hormone oozed into a large styrofoam cup. Then he wrapped the cup in a plastic bag to contain moisture.

Meanwhile, he preached the virtues of his tree. "California laurel, bay laurel, Oregon myrtle—whatever you call it, it's the finest wood in the world. But turn it over to a local woodman, and he don't know it.

"Confound it! The wood looks like curley maple or marble," he blurted. But where you gonna get a hundred board feet of that, these days? It's hard, like brass. Just look at that log I brought with me from Oregon. Took only thirty-two years for that to get a foot and a half in diameter!" Harold exclaimed.

Harold couldn't understand why the world hadn't beaten a path to his doorstep for his fast-growing, high-quality hardwood. But he was committed to keeping on, potting and tending and praying over the little forest in his backyard.

"They *can* be grown here, now that I've found the way," Harold declared with finality. "And they'll grow faster than anybody has any idea, or I'm a-sonufagun!"

Potting fresh cuttings, Harold shakes his head in wonder. "Holycheesus, but I've been through a lot."

Morris Nanney, Farmer

I did some good farming . . .

Nobody could agree on exactly how to say it. Was it "Mumford's Cove," or maybe "Munferd Cove," as most of the natives pronounced it? Most likely it was a stepchild of the proper "Montford Cove," the way it appeared on maps made by outlanders and which nobody said—leastwise, they didn't if they were from the cove.

Morris Nanney wasn't sure either, but it didn't matter. To Morris it was not how you said it, but what you knew deep down about the place that counted. The patriarch of the cove had been farming the narrow width of bottomland for the better part of his ninety years and knew it as well as—no—*better* than the back of his hand.

In the shadow of Pinnacle Mountain, Morris had lived and worked the land hard. He had farmed, logged, built his house, fought fires, registered taxes, supervised elections, taught Sunday school, dug graves, and served as church treasurer and deacon for as long as anyone could remember.

"I've worked hard all of my days. It's been many a day that me 'n' Charlie Banning'd go down in the Bird Thicket, we called it, when the sun was hot there and cut cross ties with a crosscut saw. And then we'd hew 'em out with a fallin' ax—ten apiece." Morris's lively Delft blue eyes shone brightly with remembrance, a face

Ninety-year-old farmer Morris Nanney:
"I worked hard all of my days."

worn brown and smooth as a well-used baseball glove creasing into a gentle smile.

He was born in a log cabin just south of the Whitehouse community beyond Painter's (Panther) Gap, which divided McDowell and Rutherford counties. Morris liked to talk about those pioneer times.

"I think of this a heap o' times, but my mother had a loom, and it sat beside the fireplace. I'd sit on the sill of that loom and peep out of this cat-hole that was hewed out beside the fireplace. I used to like to do that," he said, sitting cross-legged and sideways in an old ladderback chair, his strong workingman's hands holding a pair of rimless glasses.

"We kept sheep, so my mother carded and spun wool. And we raised enough cotton to make thread, so she made our blankets, clothes, and stockings. I've seen her weave many a day. Wove me a blanket I've still got.

"I re-collect my mother saying she never knowed what it was to go to the store—'cept for sugar, coffee, and rice. Stuff like that. We always raised all our own food. Had a cow for milk and butter. Always had a hog killed, canned meat for ribs, sausage, and the like."

Like most farm children raised before the turn of the century, Morris learned the meaning of hard work early. "As l growed up I soon learned to bridle the mule that we owned and would take it to the creek to get water." He laughed softly about the time he and his sister went for water and fell in. "I wanted to sit in front of her to hold the reins, but as soon as we got to the creek the mule went to drink—and we both went over his head into the creek and got a good dunking."

He attended Round Hill Academy that was a five-mile trek across the mountain in Union Mills—and then the nearby Oak Hill School in the days before tax-supported public education was available. But most of his time was taken helping his father farm, and "helping him in the shop as he did a lot of blacksmithing and wagon repair."

At the age of twenty-one, Morris married Esther Harris, and they moved in with her parents in the big two-story frame house beside the Montford Cove road where Morris would spend most of his life. Morris went into full-time farming, putting in his first crop of corn in 1913.

"Split my own wood," declares Morris.
"Never did pay to have that done."

"I did some good farming," he said, listing his progress through the teens: another crop of corn, their first-born child; another crop of corn, one of wheat—and another child. In 1915 he purchased a large, old store building for salvage and with that heart-pine lumber he built his own house.

The big flood of 1916 sent the little valley's Cove Creek boiling into the bottoms, but Morris was lucky. "The freshet of 1916 destroyed a lot of the corn, and so it was going for a good price. What I was able to save I sold for two dollars a bushel at the crib."

Later that year he decided for insurance to farm the higher ground, setting out peach trees. "I guess they were as nice peaches as were growed in McDowell County. Brought me some good money at that time—though I had to sled them off the mountain and take them to market in a stick-seated buggy."

That prompted him to buy his first car, a Model T Ford, "so that it'd holp out a lot in taking the peaches and many other vegetables to market as I did a lot of truck farming." But if Morris used a car for the rutted market road to Marion twelve miles distant, he never could see the use of a tractor.

"I traded for a big Percheron horse that I kept for many years— called him Charlie. Never did own a tractor. I just kept good horses and a ridin' plow. I raised some good crops and liked it pretty well."

In his remote community, Morris was a respected leader. "I did just a little bit of everything—was on the school committee, I holpt dig many a grave down there as long as they were dug by free labor, I was on the committee to rebuild the church after it burned in 1934, and I was the first fire warden in these parts.

"That was in the day when we had no way of traveling—only by foot and by horseback. When we'd see a smoke, we fought it with just ol' wooden rakes and when we could, we'd take the advantage and set a fire agin it."

To help make ends meet, Morris worked part-time at a department store in Marion on the weekends, "when holp got kindly hard to find during that war number two, y'know." He kept on farming and logging through the sixties until he and his wife had to go to the hospital for a number of ailments. Morris recovered from several surgeries, but his wife's condition was far more serious. After a period of decline, she died in 1968. Her passing was still a source of grief for the old man.

Cradling her portrait in his hands, he praised her memory. "She

A pigeon-holed writing desk
serves as Morris's filing system
for his correspondence and
historical research.

was a good wife and mother and a good provider. We all miss her.
It's been twelve years and a half now," he said simply.

Morris placed the picture tenderly on the top of a cubbyholed
writing desk that was fairly bursting with stacks of paper, correspondence, and his records verifying the location of an old Indian
fort in the nearby mountains.

Laying his rimless glasses on the desk beside his wife's picture,
Morris picked up a frayed Bible bound together with a generous
application of silver duct tape. He hoisted himself up carefully
and walked through the house, through the kitchen where he did
his own cooking and canning, and out to the back porch.

From there his old blue eyes squinted against the August sun as
he surveyed his rural fiefdom knowingly: A well-loaded woodshed
("Split my own wood. Never did pay to have that done."); his
sturdy, off-white Chevy II; a pair of venerable silver maples flank-
ing the house; and his neat garden with tassled corn well over
head-high. And then, holding up the old Bible with both hands as
if to personally recommend it to the visitor, he said with conviction, "Read it every day. Pray too, mister."

Part Three   Music

Well I'll tell you what buddy I cut stovewood tuned pianos took a little charity from the state like most blind folks and did a whole lot of walkin' and didn't have no car either. . . . Back in the fifties, son, I played with a country swing group. Well it put biscuits on the table and little overhawls on Merle.

—Doc Watson

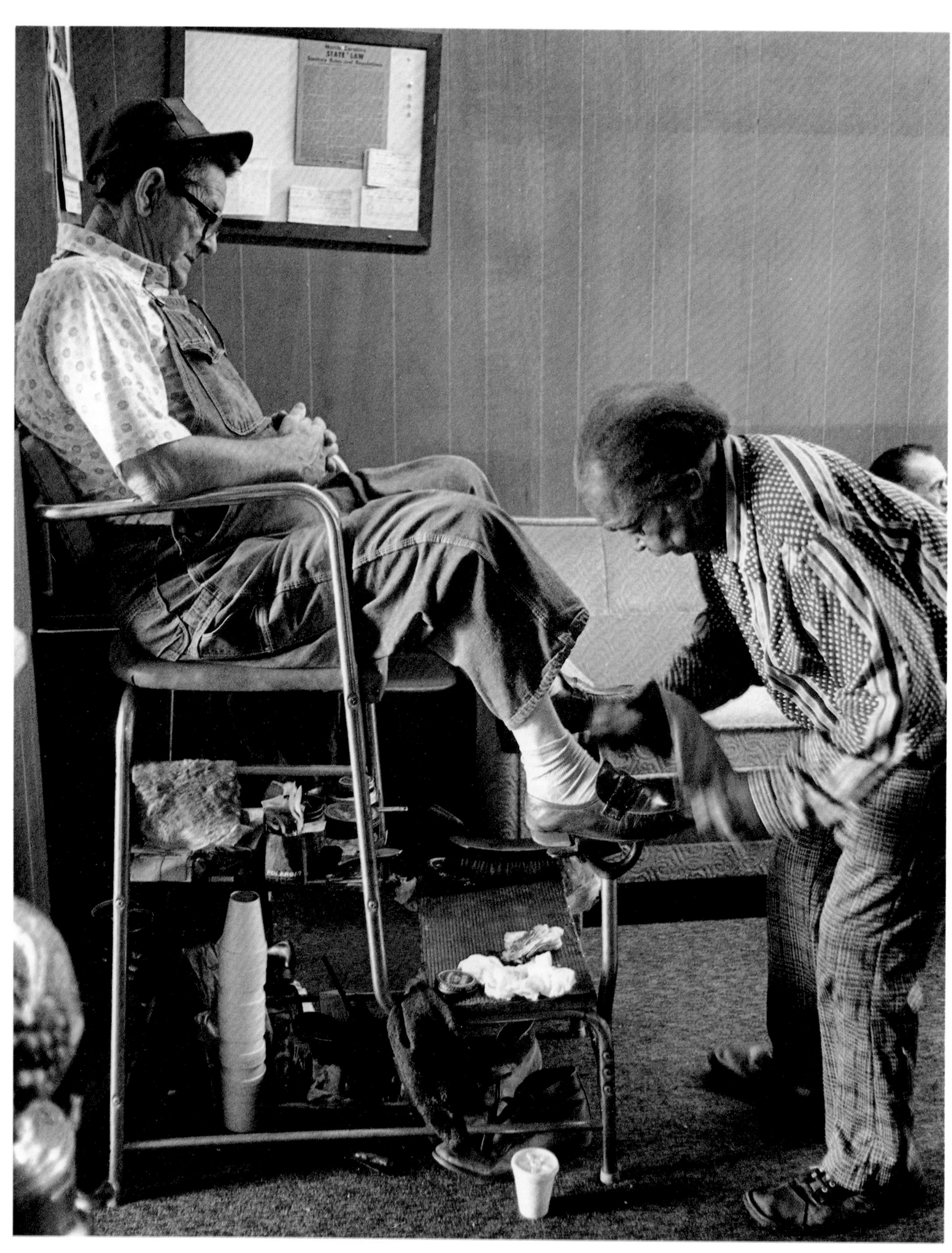

A Marion patron watches as "Rhythm Willy"
lickety-splits through a tune he calls "Trottin' Sally."

"Rhythm Willy" Shade, Shoeshine Man

Lotta changin' goin on. Yessir, an' still makin' more changes.

"**R**hythm Willy" Shade was proud that he worked at the state's oldest barbershop, even if Marion folks still persisted in calling him a "shoeshine boy."

If he minded, Willy never took offense publicly. At seventy-two, he was the oldest thing in the City Barbershop, next to the mint green Koken barber chairs and the pair of 1923 cash registers—and, of course, the shop itself, which was started there on the dusty main street in 1902 by "Handy" Bowman.

The late Jack Harris bought the shop in the late twenties, and his son Tom, who said he was practically raised in the barbershop, took over. All the while, Rhythm Willy was there. Nobody could remember exactly when Willy came to work, but he reckoned with a grin (one gold tooth gleaming prominently) he'd "been around for at least 120 years."

He wagged a bushy head frosted with the first hints of gray upward at a yellowing cardboard sign bearing his title over the elevated shoeshine chair: "Rhythm Willy—that's me."

Starting at the City Barbershop as a twelve-year-old, Willy just shined shoes the conventional way at first. Then a trip to the mountain metropolis of Asheville opened his eyes. "Got the idea of playin' the rag from a bootblack parlor in Asheville way back," he confided. "It takes a special kind of rag, though. I jus' made the tunes up. I do what I call 'Trottin' Sally,' an' 'Turkey Trot,' an' 'The Buzzard Lope.' I'm the only one who does it."

On special occasions, and when Willy knew he had an appreciative customer, he'd still play that rag. A shambling collection of plaids, stripes, and polka-dots, Willy addressed the shoe like a loose-jointed tap dancer confronting a challenging piece of ragtime choreography.

Out came the old silk rag . . . a strategic pause. Then, balancing and hopping on his splay-bottomed, red, white, and blue platform shoes, the old bootblack attacked first one shoe with gusto. "Whup-whup-whup," went the rag.

"Whuppa-*whap*"—then the other shoe got it.

"Whuppa-*whap*—

"Whuppa-*whap-whap-whap*!"

The polish-stained rag blitzed, snapped, and popped in the old man's hands expertly—he, the virtuoso on the percussion instrument of his own devising.

"That Willy can do it!" Tom Harris sang out proudly, watching from his second barber chair.

"Go, Willy!" called out a customer.

"Pop that thang just one more time!" hollered another.

The little barbershop was beginning to resemble an old-time revival meeting. Willie, gold tooth flashing like a proud star, obliged, and the staccato cadence crescendoed and climaxed with a series of loud crackles and pops.

Letting go the rag with one hand, Willy performed the last snap, flourishing the rag upward like a composer's baton signaling the final note of a crashing symphony. The roomful of patrons and barbers broke into appreciative applause, with Tom Harris bestowing the verbal roses: "See there? Willy hasn't forgotten after all."

The customer, a little dazed by the artistry of it all, lowered faded overalls over white socks, and tipped Willy a whole quarter. Willy bobbed and nodded, then took his place in the shoeshine chair, waiting for another customer. He sat there as if it were his throne while he watched the familiar parade of life in the shop.

It was a big hair-cutting day in Marion. School was out for the summer, so children and parents took seats either for trims or for witnessing. Tom Harris grinned broadly and announced in a loud sing-song, "Oh, I've uncovered a lotta ears today! A *lotta* ears."

Old and young took their turn in the venerable Koken chairs, installed on a memorable day in 1928. The local newspaper had alerted the small town about the notable addition to Main Street: "The City Barbershop on South Main will soon have five latest model Koken barber chairs for the comfort of its patrons. The chairs are looked for every day, word having been received that they've been shipped."

Tom Harris philosophized: "They cost four hundred dollars apiece then and must be about twelve to fourteen hundred dollars now. No use to replace them. They still work." About the only visible signs of wear on the chairs was the iron scrollwork on the footrests where countless thousands of footfalls had scuffed the metal to a dull sheen.

The TV chattered mindlessly some game show from atop its perch on the 'Coke machine; no one seemed to watch. The barbers' shears whined and blended musically with the transfer trucks' surflike roar on Main Street. Willy made a circuit around the three antique green chairs with a broom and a piece of cardboard, collecting the black, brown, blond, and gray hair into a multi-colored, democratic fuzzball.

The old barbershop hummed to its own pace. Folks swapped yarns, and the barbers jawed conversationally with patrons about the kids, the weather, the big layoff over at the mills. A June breeze riffled through the shop from the open back door on the alley.

Rhythm Willy surveyed the place, on the surface changed very little except for some cosmetic alterations these eighty years. The spittoons were gone, the overhead fans had been taken down, and the rough plank flooring had been covered over. But essentially, the state's oldest barbershop was still intact.

From his vantage point at the back, Willie sat beneath the sign he wore like a crown. He observed with enigmatic eyes, heavy-lidded like an old turtle's, "Lotta changin' goin' on. Yessir, an' still makin' more changes." He would be the last rag-poppin' "shoeshine boy" these parts would ever see, and he knew it.

A cacophony of plaids and polka dots,
the seventy-two-year-old rests beneath his sign.

Doc Watson, the dean of the Blue Ridge flatpickers.

Doc Watson, Folk Musician

I'm a-tellin' you—it's a God-given thing . . .

Grasping his son's strong arm, Doc Watson, sixty-two, walked with Merle in step across the wet, grassy yard. A shrouding fog enveloped the bowl-shaped mountain valley. Beside a simple frame house a large weeping willow danced in the spring wind; on the far side of the yard, a newer brick house spread.

Between the two houses—the two worlds—the two renowned musicians trod. They were used to bridging such gaps—as they did with their music, a blend of folk, country, old-time, bluegrass, pop, and country swing that defied easy pigeon-holing.

Doc (born "Arthel") was the undisputed dean of the flatpickers, the pride of Deep Gap, a man *Time* magazine had once called "perhaps the finest living American folk artist performing today." Ralph Rinzler, assistant secretary of the Smithsonian Institution, is credited with discovering Doc back in 1960 at the state's oldest fiddler's convention at Union Grove. Rinzler says Doc earned that nickname back in the early days while playing on a Lenoir radio station.

Between intensive bouts of performing on the road, Doc would retreat to the old family homeplace ten miles out of Boone. They kept the old house as a touchstone of their origins, a free-standing scrapbook that reminded them of the lean times when Merle was little and nobody had ever heard of a blind guitar-picker named Doc Watson.

Doc talked like he plays guitar—bass strings ringing lickety-split in an arpeggio of guitar notes too fast for any normal mortal to put down. He flared a sentence devoid of commas: "Well I'll tell you what buddy I cut stovewood tuned pianos took a little charity from the state like most blind folks and did a whole lot of walkin' and didn't have no car either."

One of nine children born into a mountain family, Doc was blind from birth. His father was a "plain ol' manual laborer—everything from carpentry to farming. He played some banjo, old-time music you'd call it today, but that was all we knew. When I was eleven in 1934, Pappa made me a little five-string banjo. The first song I learned I still remember. It was 'Rambling Hoboes.'"

Doc's father was determined that the blind lad learn to deal with the real world. Doc remembered the day when as a fourteen-year-old he was taken to the woodlot by his father, who put his hands on the crosscut saw and said, "Son, you *can* work."

"And you know, I *could*," Doc said.

"I was standing on the street corner of North Wilkesboro in 1952 and Whitey Grant with the Briarhoppers came along and dropped twenty-five cents in my cup and says who he is and he was a big man in country music then. Well a coupla years ago at Ben Humphrey's bluegrass festival down in Cliffside I saw Whitey Grant again and he asked me if he could have his quarter back and I told him right quick—hello no!" A Doc Watson laugh went from one side of the mountain to the other.

"Back in the fifties, son, I played with a country swing group—well it put biscuits on the table and little overhawls on Merle—and we made just a couple of shekels every week. Well I'll tell you back then you had to have a flashy show—and I ain't flashy. But in the early sixties Ralph Rinzler came down and took it upon himself to help me in the music business and I thank God for that."

Rinzler, at the time a New York music promoter, propelled Doc into popularity. Doc had recorded or been a part of nineteen albums, and had toured Japan and Europe repeatedly along with his gifted, guitar-playing son, Merle, and fiddler Mark O'Conner.

Merle, who not only could keep up with his dad on the smoking flat-picking riffs, but also managed the duo, was a seventeen-year veteran on the road with his father. Doc credited his wife, Rosalee, with teaching Merle. Lavishing praise on her, he said, "She taught him his first chords and he took it and went with it, son—he ain't no throwback neither. Hello, he's getting fine on that slide guitar. You're either born with talent or not and I'm a-tellin' you it's a God-given thing. Merle's got both—that's the love of it and the talent."

Recording and performing success had not come without sacrifices. There were some hard times Doc said he'd just as soon forget. "I could never live the sixties over again," he said frankly. "Some of it is like a nightmare. Merle would have to drive all night to get places and he'd be so beat by when we'd get there he'd have to sleep all day while I played. Well I'll tell you buddy I couldn't do that again. Lord have mercy now we fly everywhere. Just three hours today back from Chicago, now that's the way to travel. If you have to drive all over this nation it'll kill you."

His lowest ebb came "in 1963 and I was playing at a place in Philadelphia called the Second Fret. I was doing two hard weeks and the job only brought in $150 total. I had a mind to quit. I'd had it up to over my ears—but this black cook named Jerry asked me to come stay with him for a while. I told him if he'd let me pay the grocery bill for the two weeks I would. Well I'll tell you what's the truth buddy—me 'n' him sat down and had steaks every night and that was the turning point in my career 'cause son I was ready to quit.

"The good Lord made sure there was somebody special there, somebody with a good heart to take care of me 'cause I was ready to drop it right then and there."

The money had gotten better than it was then, but the Watsons continued to live modestly in their mid-size brick home in Deep Gap. The star status had not gone to this mountain man's head. "I'm satisfied," declared Doc. "I don't care about being a big star. I don't want people to worship me. I just appreciate people enjoying it if I do a good job—just like you'd compliment a carpenter or a plumber if he did a good job. But I don't want any stardom. The good Lord didn't intend people to live like that. These young men who get to be stars get up so high on it that when it all comes down they have to use liquor or drugs to keep them up and that becomes their god. Anything done in excess can become your god.

"Some of these young stars become arrogant toward the world.

What have *I* got to be arrogant about? Ask Rosalee. Sometimes I'm as ornery and no-count as can be.

"You've got to put God in his place and stardom in its place. Nobody is better than anybody else son, and I'll tell you what's the truth—that's what it's all about. One man might do something better than another man, but that's no reason him getting all puffy or self-righteous about himself."

Doc's humility was part of his honest charm as he and Merle traveled, performing about 60 percent of the time. At sixty-two, Doc was beginning to think about retirement someday. He and Rosalee were dreaming of building a new house near her homeplace there in Deep Gap where she played as a child—a place with privacy, a "nearly flat" garden for her, and a full basement for him where Doc said he wanted to produce a radio program of his collected old-time music.

Meanwhile, there was another European tour to be reckoned with, and countless numbers of performances all over the country upon his return. "I hate the traveling," Doc leveled. "But I do love to perform for two reasons: I'm doing something that people enjoy and I'm earning a living."

Doc's deep, rich baritone thrummed, "And I'll tell you what's the truth buddy—the good Lord was with me every step of the way."

ang played—plays—will always play as long as he's got a breath left in him
—the jazz rhythm guitar.

Isidore Langlois, Jazzman

See man? That's jazz.

"Jazz . . .?" the old jazzman leaned on his guitar and looked momentarily stumped. "What can I say, man? It's just something that comes natural. It's expression."

Isidore Langlois, seventy-three, looked out of the window as if searching for a vision. "Look, it's like this: the guys can be together and one of 'em might look out the window and see a bird fly past. Well, there's a rhythm right there . . ."

"Lang," as he is called, poised over his guitar and began singing, snapping his fingers and bouncing on the couch all at once:

> There's the blue bird,
> Lookit him fly;
> There's the bluebird,
> Lookit him fly;
> He ain't goin' nowhere, nowhere,
> He ain't goin' nowhere.

"And then the rest of the cats, they'd be goin', 'da-da-da, dee-dee-dee, da-da-da, dee-dee-dee.'" Lang looked up triumphantly, spread his arms wide, and smiled. "See man? *That's* jazz."

The old jazzman lived in Tryon where he worked as a cook and still played jazz guitar for special occasions. He was born in Harlem to parents of French extraction from Martinique, and jazz was his playmate. "I was halfway sharp," he joked, sitting in his basement music den in his home in Polk County surrounded by forty years of memorabilia: old guitars, a frowzy dartboard, a silver ceremonial sword, Caribbean carvings, a set of old pottery, goatskin bongo drums, out-of-print books, 78 rpm Bluebird records, an autographed baseball bat, baseball bubblegum cards, several pictures of the Virgin Mary and one of Louis Armstrong.

Lang played—plays—will always play as long as he's got a breath left in him—the jazz rhythm guitar. Back in the thirties when jazz was being born in the clubs of Harlem, Lang was there with a six-piece combo.

Listing Lang's musical history sounds like the combined volumes of *Who's Who in American Jazz* and *Europe on $25 a Day*. Lang and his band were given a contract to play at the top jazz spots of Europe, including "Du Hot Club De France" and "Chez Florence" in Paris where Lang said Marlene Dietrich was a frequent guest. When the group, "The Harlem Hot-Shots," broke up, Lang stayed on with the Eddie South band touring to Amsterdam. South, Lang recalled, was nicknamed "the Dark Angel of the Violin."

He returned to the States in the jazzy thirties and continued a career that would bring him into contact with many of the major jazz greats of that golden era: Billie Holiday, Fats Waller, Willie "The Lion" Smith, Fletcher Henderson, Louis Armstrong, George Gershwin, Charlie Shavers, Art Tatum, and Django Reinhardt, to name a few.

"I remember it was the Depression," Lang said, "and Billie Holiday had done an all-night gig at the Alhambra Theater in Harlem. That would be at 7th Avenue and 126th Street. Nobody was making any money—but everybody was happy. Billie Holiday was singing for *peanuts.* . . . *I* was working for peanuts. I walked her home after that gig.

"When Billie's father got sick, they called me to take his place in the Fletcher Henderson band, probably the greatest band in existence at that time."

Lang played for a while with the Henderson group, but became ill in Chicago. "It just all came down on me," he said mournfully. "I told Fletcher I was gonna visit my mother and father in Chicago and rest for a while. Then after that, I started giggin' around Chicago and never rejoined the band."

Some of Lang's jazz memories stand alone as pie-slices from the thirties. He recollected vividly when he was hired to play music for gangsters. "I remember the time I was standing outside the

"Lang" cherishes a memento of his jazz days in Paris.

Musicians' Club in Harlem and these gangster-type gentlemen in wide-brim hats and driving a Cadillac touring car drove up. They said, 'We're gonna have a racket over in Jersey tonight. Can you boys give us some noise?'

Lang shook his head. "They called it '*noise.*' Anyway, we got in and they drove us way up the Jersey coast, back into the woods to an old log cabin. Well, we played all night, and about four o'clock I said to my partner I'd go get the pay. They had told me at the end of the night just ask for the 'Doctor.' So I went over to the bartender and said, 'Say man, where's the Doctor?'

"'Who's sick?,' said the bartender.

"'Nobody's sick. I just want my money.'

"'Ain't no doctors here,' said the bartender.

"So I went over to one of the waiters. 'Hey man, which dude's the Doctor 'round here?' I said.

"'Who's sick?' says the waiter. "Well, I was getting tired of this—so I looked around for the guys who'd hired us and they were gone! Man, they'd hired us to play all night, and we didn't get a dime. Hot-dem!" Lang exploded with a gust of laughter.

"I'm *still* trying to collect for that night. We had to pass the hat among the waiters to get back to New York City. Holy cow, that was a gangster hangout."

Lang recounted also how jazz musicians would gather in Harlem clubs and play all night just for the sheer delight of it. There was a certain pecking order that determined which musicians got to play what.

"Willie 'The Lion' Smith used to come in with a cigar stuck in the corner of his mouth, and thump the dude on the piano on the shoulder and say, 'Hey boy, let a *man* play the piano.' Shoot! The guy would jump up. Willie Smith was a bad man on the piano. That's how come he was called that. He was the *lion* of the piano. He was baaaa-aaad. But then, if Fats Waller came in, Willie Smith'd get up. That's how it used to be, man."

Another experience Lang liked to tell about: it was the late thirties and at a private party at a plush Park Avenue address the guest list included the celebrities of the day—Paul Whiteman, Harold Arlen, Babe Livingston, George Gershwin, and more.

"Willie 'The Lion' Smith was on one piano and Fats Waller on the other one; baby grands—back-to-back. Goldie Lucas on one guitar and me on the other. Twin pianos and two guitars. Don't you think we made some sounds?

"Then George Gershwin and Fats did a duet you'd never forget. What a night that was. Nobody thought about recording anything. I don't even think the tape recorder was invented yet. Nobody thought it was that special. It was just the popular music of the time. Bee-bop wasn't invented yet, and there was none of this rock and roll. It was just plain jazz—Gershwin and jazz.

"Yeah, I knew Louis. We played together back in Chicago at the Dreamland Café on State and 35th streets at the time when Louis Armstrong wasn't making any money. He didn't make any money until he went to New York City.

"I remember the time Louis and I had a recording session together for the Norge refrigerator people. That's when I found out Aunt Jemima was a white woman.

"Louis'd say, 'Aunt Jemima, what I want to know is—how big is a Norge refrigerator?'"

Lang was doing his throaty Louis Armstrong impersonation and having a great time of it: "'Well Aunt Jemima, it's gotta be big enough to hold a watermelon.'

"'Oh Louis,' Aunt Jemima'd say, 'A Norge refrigerator is big enough to hold *two* watermelons.'

"'That's all I wanted to know. All I wanted to know.'" Satchmo's sandpaper basso voice was perfectly duplicated, and Lang shook his head, laughing to himself, "Oh boy."

"You know, Louis never wanted to be a star. He didn't consider himself a vocalist. He just wanted to play his horn.

"You don't live very long, man. 'Cause once you become a star, you gotta live that way. Louis just wanted to play that horn. That's the way I feel about it. Just play my instrument and maybe earn a buck here and there." Lang quickly tuned the electric Guild jazz guitar and began playing Rodgers and Hart's "The Lady Is a Tramp."

The old jazzman's musical gait, his transfixed face, and nimble brown fingers all combined to capture the essence of the music of the thirties. As his friend and Rutherfordton jazzist Louis Deviney said of Isidore Langlois: "This cat's a walking, talking, playing history book."

Lang wound up the song with an augmented seventh chord and rocked back on the couch with an easy grin of accomplishment. "You know what they say about old jazz musicians?" He rested both arms on the guitar's side. "Old jazzmen never die, they just play away. Yessir, they just play away."

Frank Swann: "Anybody who's going to own that fiddle's going to have Epps blood."

Frank Swann and the
Family Fiddle

I'm as independent as a pig on ice.

That old Epps fiddle would forever remain in the family—if Frank Swann had anything to say about it.

Frank, "eighty-five if I live to April," sat back in his recliner, folded his hands, closed his eyes, and began conjuring up the saga of the Epps family fiddle. "It began like this: Uncle Passon Epps— we called him Uncle Pass—he had this old fiddle. Nobody knows how old it was because he had it before the Civil War, and he was too old I imagine to go to war, so the fiddle had to be pretty old by the time the war come around—when was that? 1861?

"Well, I learned about it all when I was a little feller sitting by my mother. Uncle Pass was her uncle. She told me about it. It was as the Civil War was ending, and the Yankees was passing through here going north, I reckon, and this feller named Palmer aimed to give them a hard time, so he cut down a bunch of trees in the road to block their way. Made them Yankees mad. So they cut back around to come another way, and they were mad. They'd steal a man's stock, kill his chickens, steal his meat, destroy his corn, and try to burn the house if they could.

"Over at the Epps house, a big ol' two-story log house in the Chapel Hill community, Uncle Pass decided he'd have to hide that fiddle—he thought so much of it. So he took a step in the stairs and hid that fiddle under the tread. Then he put the board back, same nails in the same holes—and them Yankees never did suspect nothing. And that's how come that fiddle escaped those Yankees.

"Now after the war, Uncle Pass's first wife she died. He married again and this woman she had a sorry brother and after Uncle Pass died this brother he took possession of the fiddle. And after a while he sold it to ol' man John Poteat—called him Fiddlin' John. There was so many Johns in the Poteat line that they had to put a tag on the different ones so to know who it was you were talking about. Yeah, Fiddlin' John.

"Now ol' man John Poteat was so particular he wouldn't let anyone mess with his fiddle, ol' man John Poteat didn't," Frank caught his breath, readjusted himself in the chair and mentally began circling the saga like a dog maneuvering around a blanket to get his bed just right. When he was ready Frank resumed: "Ol' man John Poteat he was a *fiddlin' man*. When my daddy was young and in his frolickin' days, the fiddle was the one that made the music in these parts. Ol' man John Poteat's son could play the banjo and his daughter could play the organ. (She's living yet; name's Ethel Toney.) Now that ol' man could make music. They could play that ol' mountain country music. 'Lexington Murder,' they used to do. And 'Devil in the Rye,' that was a fast fiddle tune. Or, 'Long-Eared Mule,' you get a good band playin' 'Long-Eared Mule,' for a square dance—whew—they can do all night!

"I'm a shut-in here. Can't even walk hardly, but if I was to hear that ol' 'Long-Eared Mule,' I'd almost have to get up and dance—or if I didn't then my legs could almost feel myself doin' it," Frank smiled ruefully.

"We'd go over there to Fiddlin' John's place over towards Pleasant Hill Church and when I had permission, we'd stay to the wee hours—way late—ol' man John Poteat didn't care; he'd play as long as you'd listen.

"And I've heard my daddy tell about the Serenades. Y'know, they'd go marching around some newlyweds or old folks' house, my daddy and the gang, all fiddling and making music. Used to have fun and big times. About the time they got around the house one time, the folks'd open the door and they'd all come in, treat 'em to apples, chestnuts, and such, and then they'd make more music and dance and carry on. They used to serenade people for a treat like that back at the turn of the century. I was in a serenade just once," he added self-consciously. "Don't believe there was any music; just shooting and cowbells. I was so ashamed of the noise we made I never did do it again."

Frank continued, "But back to the Epps fiddle: ol' man John Poteat he knowed that fiddle belonged to my people; my grandmother was an Epps—Uncle Pass's sister. I decided when I was a little feller that I wanted to get that fiddle. But I was young and it was hard times, too. It was many a times that I'd walk to town and dig ditches for twenty-five cents a day to feed my family.

"In ol' man John Poteat's last days I believe if I'd gone to him he'd a-give me that fiddle, 'cause he told Mrs. Smith his sister that he wanted me to have it. But when he passed on, the fiddle went to his son, Johnny, a good friend of mine.

"Now Johnny was a *dollar* man, and one day I saw him at the bank and asked him what he'd take for it, and Johnny said he'd have to ask his folks. A month later I saw him at the bank again and asked him, 'How 'bout that fiddle?' and he made me a price. I made him a down payment and got that old fiddle. A year later he was killed in a car wreck. I come just that nigh to losing that ol' fiddle. That was about 1961. I know I got that fiddle just in time.

"It had a homemade case made out of three-quarter-inch board lined with red plush. Now it was *fixed up*. But it looked just like a baby casket. Didn't have no handle, it was just an ol'-time homemade job. When I'd carry it around under my arm, I'd have to tell folks it wasn't a baby casket," Frank laughed.

Frank didn't consider himself much of a musician. "If I heard a tune in my mind, then I could play it. But I'm not a fiddler, no." And after a while he quit fiddling entirely. He was just content to keep the precious Epps fiddle "in a secluded place," he said secretively. But as the years went by, Frank began worrying about the fate of the fiddle. "Then, that second boy of mine, Donald, he asked me to will him the fiddle. That was a right smart time ago. He's a farmer down in Texas. Farms nineteen hundred acres.

"Well he was coming up here for Christmas this year, so instead of willing it to him, I decided he should have some pleasure out of that ol' fiddle while I was still alive. So after all the gifts were opened, I went and got that fiddle and gave it to him under one condition: that fiddle is going to stay in our family. Anybody who's going to own that fiddle's going to have Epps blood. Now that's how sentimental and independent I am about it. I'm just as independent as a pig on ice. Yeah, you ever seen a pig on ice? Then you know how I am. There's no way you could put a price tag on that fiddle. Money don't count.

"My son says he's taking that fiddle back to Texas and putting it up in a trophy case—just the way it is. It even had a homemade screw in it ol' man James Poteat made. My son says he's going to leave it just like that.

"He's having his lawyer fix up a paper saying that when he passes on then the fiddle goes to one of his daughters, and if they have children then it goes to them. If they don't have children then it comes back here to my other grandchildren. It can't go to a wife of a husband. It's going to stay in the family. I had too hard a time getting that fiddle back to lose it again," Frank declared.

"Everyone who's ever played that fiddle says it's the sweetest fiddle they've ever played. Fiddles now, they're not like singers. If a singer quits singing then it'll take him awhile to get his voice back in shape. But a fiddle, the more you play it, the sweeter it sounds."

Part Four   Animals

I'd die for my bears this evening. Well, I would! If they was to come get my bears, they'd have to kill me first. That's how much I love my bears. I love 'em just like a man loves his children.
                                        —Emmett Gray

Nelle Smith and Roscoe the Groundhog

That must be groundhog love . . .

Nelle Smith had a woodchuck that lived in her washing machine. She was fond of saying that "with Roscoe, every day is Groundhog Day."

Lifting the chubby groundhog out of the kitchen trash can, Nelle asserted proudly, "Roscoe's *all* groundhog." As if to demonstrate just what an accepted family member he was, Roscoe began tearing about the Gilkey community log house with the abandon of a strapping two-year-old.

First, he started boxing with Nelle's two poodles, Kimberly and Casey-J. Then in a bound, he was up on the kitchen table munching a banana briefly. Next, on his stubby legs he waddled hastily to the back porch to defiantly swat over the dog food bag. Finally Roscoe visited the bathroom where he gnawed happily on the soap and lathered up his short tail (a favorite trick).

Nelle just smiled like the patient mother she was to the spoiled marmot. "He likes to tear things up, so you just pick it up and smile. What else can you do?" Nelle said patiently. After sixteen years with Roscoe, she was used to his antics.

She had found him on a wildflower hunt over in neighboring Polk County. "The li'l pig was next to death. I found him a-layin' in the dirt road. Couldn't a-been over three weeks old—all wet and covered with flies. He was in sad shape. Reckon his mother was killed by dogs.

"I just had a desire to see if I could make that little thing live—and I did. I went straight to the store and bought a nursin' bottle. But heck—the nipple was bigger'n his head. Then I took a medicine dropper and gave him four bottles full of milk that first time. I stopped because I didn't know how much to give him. . . . Well, he just sat right up in my hand and started lickin' and cleanin' himself up."

Looking at the sleek, well-fed creature larger than any alley-bred tomcat, Nelle conceded it was hard for her to imagine Roscoe as ever being runty. But Nelle said she had to feed Roscoe four times a day and night with the medicine dropper until he was old enough to grapple with the baby bottle by himself. When he finally grew up, Roscoe satisfied himself with a banana a day, a pimento cheese sandwich ("His favorite," Nelle said), and—if he could get the lid off—an entire jar of mayonnaise.

"He's a cure-osity, all right," Nelle proclaimed proudly as Roscoe busily skittered from the back porch to the bedroom. "We call him 'li'l pig' because groundhogs are called 'whistlin' pigs' sometimes. He just chuckle and whistle like a man if he a-wants to."

The woodchuck, which gets its name from a Cree Indian word, "wuchak," usually hibernates all winter. According to an old Germanic and Anglo-Saxon legend, the animal comes out on Candlemas Day, February 2, an Anglican and Catholic holy day, to bless the next year's candles for church use. Thus the groundhog is supposed to emerge from his den to fulfill the old rhyme:

> If Candlemas is fair and clear
> There'll be two winters in the year.

Folks in Rutherford County had heard of the national groundhog, Punxsutawney Phil, up in Pennsylvania. But the locals were not impressed. Said a "Yankee groundhog" had no business prognosticating weather south of the Mason-Dixon line—especially in the hill country.

So Roscoe had become something of a local celebrity. Nelle reported, acting playfully peeved at all the notoriety, "I've had people I didn't even know come up to me and ask, 'How's Roscoe?' They don't even ask how *I* am—they just want to know how Roscoe is . . ."

Years back, the first time Roscoe went into his winter hibernation, Nelle and her son Timmy were sure he had died. Nelle recalled Timmy saying, 'We better get Roscoe to the vet,' but then
Nelle slowly began to realize what was happening—and laughed
with relief. "Son, you take that ol' groundhog to Dr. Cline, and
he'll run us off!"

From then on, each winter Roscoe would bed down in an abandoned washing machine out in an outhouse where he "looked
about dead. They say they're just one heartbeat away from death—
he's so cold," she said with a shiver. "It's that deep sleep that leaves
'em cold as death."

One year Roscoe had gone to sleep in December, and Nelle said
he had been "dead-cold as a block of ice." Then on the night of
February 1, he awoke without any prodding and they heard him at
the backdoor, "raising all kind of Cain to come in. . . . So I let him
in, and he had a big cut-up, ran and played and rassled with the
dogs. He was so happy to see us."

Curiously, the next year, Roscoe did little or no hibernating.
Nelle speculated it was because Roscoe was forgetting his roots.
"See, Roscoe never knew nothin' but people, and he's never seen
another groundhog, so he don't know what he is. He thinks he's
people probably," she said. "Oh, he's lived high on the hog."

Roscoe, ignoring such talk, rummaged through the closet, then
without warning rocketed across the living room floor and jumped
on the couch with an agility that belied his bulk.

"Rossi, where you goin', boy?" Nelle chatted comfortably with
the bodacious creature. "I've told him many a time that the reason
his mama left him was because he was so wild. Yup, I've told him
that many a-time . . ."

In response, Roscoe vaulted into Nelle's lap, ignoring the poodle
already there. Yawning and stretching, he plopped down luxuri-
ously with what looked like a satisfied smirk.

Nelle smiled down at the furry bundle in her lap. "So long as he
stays with me he's not gonna be underfed or underloved. Sometimes he'll just crawl up here and rub his ol' face on mine. I guess
he's a-lovin' me; that must be groundhog love."

Inspecting Pearl's teeth while Nancy watches,
Howard McKinney says he's "been foolin' with mules for fifty years."

Howard McKinney
and His Mules

Nothin' beats a mule.

The January ground was frozen like a brick in a deep freeze. Even meandering McCanless Creek stayed iced over by midday. Inside the heart-pine McKinney house, a crackling chestnut oak fire drew visitors to its beckoning warmth—the sole source of heat in the old farmhouse. Too cold to plow, reckoned Howard McKinney, but never too cold to praise mule power.

"Nothin' beats a mule," Howard preached, rocking back precariously in his chair and slinging his right leg over the arm rest. "A mule's just as fur ahead of horses as can be—as fur as farmin' goes."

Howard was not speaking out of turn. Far beyond his own creekside farm in McDowell County, he was known as the area's most expert mule man. Howard, who didn't give his age, was sure he'd "been foolin' with mules for fifty years," and he could be seen regularly turning folks' gardens along Ashworth Road when the soil, season, and moon were right.

Around the fire sat Irvin Hyde, Denver Randolph, and Howard's sister Gardie. The loose semi-circle of ladderbacks and rockers was pulled as close to the fire as was deemed safe. The talk ranged from mules to the weather to old times: things the foursome knew well.

Howard chewed on a homemade toothpick and scanned a newspaper. There was a photograph of a political candidate passing through Marion in a mule-drawn wagon. Howard was impressed. Pointing at the picture, he exclaimed, "Now, *them's* some good-lookin' mules." The other men bent forward to inspect the photo, ignoring, like Howard, the politician's fatuous grin. "That white around the mouth and eyes and nose—that there's the makin' of a good mule. Yeh!"

A good mule was the measure of the man, Howard believed. "Ain't hard to plow with a mule if you know how to. If you grip that plow and fight it, you'll have a hard time. Everything's knowin' what to do. Why, I can just lay a finger on the plow and go along. Don't try to manhandle it; just let the mule turn around by themselves. Some people are so mean to their stock that they won't mind 'cause they be so afraid. And y'gotta be careful on stumpy land. If you're not—them plow handles'll kick your ribs in.

"Sometimes the hardest mule to break is the best mule there are. And you don't have to ask a mule to pull—'cause that's his nature. He don't want to be outdone. There was this eye-talian feller I logged for who was always amazed how a mule'd pull; there ain't no *makin'* to it. Now take Ol' Mary—she was the free-est pullin' mule I ever owned—she and Ol' Beck. Why, they would solid *pull*," Howard avowed.

Howard said, "The day was when a man didn't mind traveling as far as Hick'ry in a wagon to pick up a good mule. The best mules came out of Tennessee, but G. C. McDaniels down in Forest City used to have a sight of good mules." Howard got his first mule from Anderson Romine down in Glenwood in the late twenties. "My father kept a awful ol' pluggy stock," Howard said unabashedly. "So I went and got my own. I was just a young feller, but in the spring o' the year I'd have fifty dollars in my pocket plantin' corn and loggin'. I got seventeen dollars a day loggin' way back when seventeen dollars meant something. Logged over on what they called Habersham Mountain. That was the best ol' loggin' mountain." Howard arched his eyebrows, then fell silent for a spell.

The fire rustled. Overhead, Gardie's quilt frame swayed slightly from hooks in the golden pine ceiling. On the far wall hung a crayon-on-cardboard portrait of a mule. Gardie had done it for Howard, and it had tickled the old mule man. A plaintive clucking from a box by the fire prompted Gardie to reveal a startled-looking game

By the fireside, sister Gardie reads the paper
while Howard discusses mule lore;
on the wall hangs a crayon picture of a mule
Gardie did for Howard.

chicken. Gardie plucked the hen from the box. "So cold outside; afraid it'd freeze to death last night. Turn her out in the daytime," she said, taking the hen to the back porch.

The men around the fire were concerned about the dry summer and fall. Howard said, "The wagon tires goes to gettin' loose when it gets dry like this." And Denver added that he wished he'd left his "longhandles" on. Pointing to his corduroy jacket, flannel shirt, overalls, and long underwear, Howard responded, "I'd rather work in the cold than the hot. I can always put more clothes on. But I can't stand it when it's unreasonable hot and you can't see for the sweat.

"Gardie says she likes the winter, and I asked her why, an' she said, ''Cause it's *interestin'*,' an' I asked her what was so interestin' about it—an' she said, ''Cause we *survived*.'" Howard grinned and then added, "But I'll tell you boys, if everything went perfect you wouldn't know how to enjoy good times. No, you wouldn't."

The talk turned to wild mules they'd known. Howard told about "Ol' man Will Turner's mule," which broke loose and "run up on the porch of the house, broke down the door, run through the house, out the kitchen, and jumped through the window. Boy, that was some high-strung mule," Howard exclaimed. "If mine were to start off somewhere, you just as well better not try to head 'em off." And that prodded Denver into recollecting the time he was riding in the back of Howard's wagon coming down the hill toward the McKinney place, "an' those mules started trottin', pickin' up speed, an' throwin' up gravel plumb up on the house. By the time we passed here we were a-flyin'—and I jumped out the back . . ."

Howard picked up the story there: "An' I didn't get 'em stopped till I got to Gus Swann's place up by the main road. I was wonderin' why you hadn't said nothin', I's too busy to turn around till I got 'em stopped—and when I did—you wasn't there no more!"

When the laughter subsided, someone noticed an old photograph hanging on the wall. It was of a whiskered gentleman standing in front of a cabin with a proud, severe-looking woman at his side. Two children in the foreground gaped curiously at the camera. Howard said the old man was his grandfather McKinney who had thirty-five brothers. When nobody in the room believed that number, Howard set into telling about his great-grandfather, the prolific Charlie McKinney. "My people come from Ireland, and Charlie McKinney had about a dozen women, I reckon. Bore him thirty-five sons, and some daughters too. He'd live with one

Late afternoon shadows stretch across the road as Howard takes a neighbor boy for a ride.

woman for a while and help her put out a crop, and go on to the next. One time I heard tell that one of his women called for him 'cause a panther was on her porch, lickin' up the pots and pans. That was up in the mountains from here. People said they envied him, seeing the Blue Ridge in its peak, before all that big timber was cut. One of his sons was Jason McKinney—the stoutest man that was ever raised on the face of the Blue Ridge mountains."

By and by, the men got up slowly from the fireside and excused themselves as the mailman came by. They ducked under Gardie's quilt frame and braced themselves for the cold that met them on the front porch. In the driveway sat Howard's well-worn mule wagon, part of which used to be bright red but was now a soft russet.

His company gone, Howard patted the side of the serviceable vehicle. "Never had an automobile. I used to go everywhere in this wagon. Hauled everything, went to town and back in it. Even hauled stuff for other people. Got apples for one feller, and I'd eat one or two. He quit lettin' me haul for him when he found out I was eatin' his stuff. He was pretty close that-a-way. This wagon can carry a full cord of green pine—and it'll just walk away with fifty-two hunnerd pounds," Howard bragged. "If it's wet you can't get a pickup truck in the woods—but you can go up there in a wagon with mules—and tie a log on the back to hold you back when you're comin' down."

Howard turned and plodded up the twining road past a collection of outbuildings, shadowed by a fuzzball of a little dog Howard called "th' Ol' Bum." Stopping by a double-sided log barn he had built as a young man, Howard recounted, "Reckon I'm the only feller around who can still hew a log. When I was young, I clumb right up there and notched with the old men. Used a plane ax. I'd notch with the best of 'em. Used to have what we called 'workin's.' Men'd gather and build a log barn or house."

Past icy McCanless Creek, under the gangly fruit trees, sat Howard's stock barn. Plainly proud of his "cow palace," Howard said, "When you see outbuildings like this on an ol' farm, you know they didn't just jump up there and get built by themselves." The place was redolent with the honest smell of farm animals. Turning to a wall where the mule bridles hung, Howard said, "After my wife died I went to courtin' a little bit. Used this one for my gal friends that liked to ride. It's solid leather. None of that ol' make-believe stuff."

Howard opened the stall and let out his team—Nancy and Pearl, great, stout beasts with large, kind brown eyes. "Yeah, they're *built*," he declared with relish. "A mule's kinda like people. Some of 'em are able to work longer than others. I heard tell of a white mule that was still plowin' gardens at forty-two. But gen'lly a hard-working mule is shot at thirty years old.

"Mine are twelve years old. Got 'em together from Madison County. You can gen'lly tell a mule's age by his mouth. Teeth'll get to stickin' plumb out, and they get a full mouth when they turn six years old. Then there's a pith that grows out right smart. Also, his jaws'll get sharp when he's old. See? They're still full and rounded on mine."

He said he was looking forward to spring, and breaking new ground again with Pearl and Nancy. "I used to plow thirty-five to forty gardens. And when I was a young feller, why—I's so tough and stout I'd go plow six or seven gardens a day. But that was way years ago. Yeah, I been old all my life. I just had a lotta miles on me. There ain't many old-timers like me left to tell us who was kin to who."

Shadowed by "the Ol' Bum,"
Howard heads for the mule barn.

Turning the mules into the pasture, Howard watched them gambol about. "Farming's gone to the bad even with tractors. But a dollar a bale of hay sure beats a dollar a gallon of gas. Ol' man Marvin Shirlin said that the land used to be so rich that you could take your straw hat and throw it on top of the wheat and it'd be so stout that your hat'd stand on the wheat."

The sky had clouded over, and January's chill nipped at the old man's bones as he walked back to the house. Howard hefted a pair of logs from a stack on the front porch, toted them inside, and resumed his vigil by the fire. "Reckon I'll haul some wood latter part of this week," said the old mule man, installing a fresh log on the glowing fire.

"That ol' chestnut oak bark burns good, don't it? Some folks grumble that I orta get me a stove—I know it'd keep me warmer." Howard grinned sheepishly. "But I just like that ol'-time way a livin'."

Emmett Gray, the Bearman
of Lake James

Oh, those bears and I have had a time.

"I just thank the good Lord for people who'll help a poor ol' raggedy country boy have what he wants and needs," Emmett Gray said humbly. But the wants and needs of the Bearman of Lake James were unlike those of most folks—as his sobriquet suggested.

He lived with three bears back on the wild side of Lake James. "I'm born and bred to it," the swarthy woodsman said emphatically, taking his ease in the front yard to escape the heat of the summer day. Over his head in an oak tree a gobbler turkey teeter-tottered huffily. A dog flopped on a bare spot by the front steps. Kittens lolled in the grass. And away up in the woods Ella Mae, Sally, and Sam rattled about their big cage restlessly.

"My granddaddy on my daddy's side had five bears at his place. He just loved bears—and he loved wildlife." Emmett sounded as if he were reciting his own eulogy. The sixty-five-year-old self-made naturalist had been keeping bears for twenty years and hunting bruins since he was eight.

"Sure! I remember that day as vivid as when it happened. Went up in Linville Gorge; camped for a week." He listed the names of the Grays and Dellingers included on that first hunt. "Didn't get nothin', but it was a thrill for me just the same," Emmett said.

With a wriggling granddaughter in his lap,
Emmett Gray says, "Oh, those bears and I have had a time."

That first hunt was just one of many for the stout farmer. "There's not been many a rock on Linville Mountain that hasn't known the feel of my feet. Why, I been all over these ol' hills."

He became seriously concerned about the dwindling bear population back in the fifties when "me 'n' a bunch of ol' country boys we seen if we didn't do something for our bear population they'd be in trouble. Whenever I's a child we could go to the mountains and we'd see bears. Then after a time, with all the hunting and logging, they began to get scarce. We decided to try and buy bears and then release them for restocking."

Reconciling how he could raise bears and then hunt them to the death was a contradiction that didn't bother Emmett. "A bear hunter enjoys keeping bears and restocking the woods to have something to hunt for, first of all. When you turn 'em loose and the dogs have treed one, at five months old, you don't know if it's one of yours.

"Just to show you how smart they are, there's this one bear we know of that goes and holes up with her cubs during hunting season in an old barn. When we go hunting we kindly lean to her a bit; she produces us two cubs every other year."

Emmett found his bears in Indiana while working construction. A small park wanted to sell its three bears because they had grown too big and rambunctious. "I drove one thousand miles twice from here up there to get the bears, me 'n' the boys. And then I started raisin' bear!" Emmett threw back the soiled bill of his John Deere cap and grinned broadly.

"I'd die for my bears this evening. Well, I would! If they was to come get my bears, they'd have to kill me first. That's how much I love my bears. I love 'em just like a man loves his children."

They tried to take his bears away from him once—in 1975 when the State Wildlife Commission ruled that people like Emmett couldn't keep wild animals in pens. But Emmett said he pitched a fit, and the flap was settled when the county commissioners declared Emmett's place the "McDowell County Zoo." Emmett said he always welcomed visitors, so the ruling really didn't change anything except that it got the bureaucratic heat off him. "My bears don't cost the taxpayers a dime—and never have." He leaned forward in his chair, china-blue eyes flashing with conviction. "Fact is, I could raise five or six fattening hogs a year on the corn alone I feed 'em. Cost-es me fifteen hunnert dollars cash money to keep 'em a year. But it's worth it to me because my grandson and any

Emmett gently delivers a gumdrop
and gets a kiss in exchange from his bear Sam.

number of other little boys can come here and have the privilege of seeing these bears—or go out and hunt 'em. I'd rather have my boys out on the lake or up in the woods than down in one of them slop-holes a-drinkin'. Now that's just the way I feel about it. To kill his first deer or bear—that just puts something in a man that nothin' else don't.

"Why, I get as much a kick out of killing a bear as I ever did when I was young. But I'd rather see a young kid kill a bear now. We got two twins that lives with us two-thirds of the time. Not ours, but those of some folks we're helpin' out. They'll be ten this next year. We just sorta annexed 'em. I'd like to take 'em on a sure-nuff bear hunt this fall. To see those boys kill a bear—that'd be the greatest thing in my whole life.

"I went on a hunt down east recently and saw an old feller,

eighty-six-year-old Pappy Burns, who's been hunting all his life, kill his first bear. And I saw a young boy and then a one-armed man kill a bear. . . . The killing of that bear put something in me that'll never get out." Emmett's big face was radiant. "What a joy I got out of seeing that.

"When the pack heads out at daylight—eight or ten dogs have give chase—why, it puts a thrill in you. And then the shot followed by the signal shot that means there's meat on the ground." Emmett beamed like a boy. "I just can't hardly wait from one fall to another to get back into it."

Raising bears had not been easy for Emmett—emotionally as well as financially. "Had one die on us. Gave Sandy too much honey. Took him to Dr. Lind. She said, 'He'll be dead before you get home. There's nothing I can do.' That cub died a-setting on my chest. We just cried like we'd lost one of our own children," Emmett said, thumbing through a scrapbook tracing the twenty-year odyssey of bear-raising. When he got to the place where Sandy died of an overdose of honey, Emmett pointed to snapshots the family had taken: of his wife, daughter Debra, and finally Emmett himself tearfully embracing the dead cub. "Oh, it tore our hearts out," Emmett said softly.

Other snapshots showed family members in various bear-hugs and receiving kisses from the bears. There was a picture of Ella Mae demolishing a very first birthday cake. "Oh, those bears and I have had a time. It's been many a night at one or two o'clock that I've had to come out here and climb that there poplar tree and get the cubs outa there. Without they got a mother, they'll just climb up there and not know how to get down. They'll just stay up there and perish to death. An old mother bear'd scare 'em down—but instead, I had to do the job."

Walking up toward the bear cage, Emmett counseled evenly, "I'm just a little juberous about going in there when they're all in there together breeding."

So he stayed outside and passed brightly colored gumdrops through the mesh wire. Ella Mae, "twenty-one years old come cubbin' time in February," tenderly took the proffered goodies from her master.

Emmett looked upon his bears as his life's work. Watching the three bears roving about their woodland habitat, he said philosophically, "I want to leave my mark somewheres along the way. Maybe the youngsters will remember ol' Paw-Paw for his bears."

Part Five   **Places**

*Creed Wilkins's Acme Service Station was dying, but the old men
pretended not to notice. . . . An October breeze bathed the Acme
with a pungent hint of woodsmoke, making the broad, dried leaves
flutter fitfully like a church full of funeral home fans.*
> **—Creed Wilkins's Acme Service Station**

An old crank phone on the wall,
the pitted pine floors, the candy counters bolted together:
very little has changed over the years
at J. Lewis Hardin's store in Shingle Hollow.

J. Lewis Hardin's Store

That's right, he could do anything, bub.

Hardin's store was not haunted; not by haints at least.
But the place was decidedly under the spell of a benevolent old spirit whose presence hung over the Shingle Hollow store as surely as the mists and fog banks that clambered over the crags of nearby Pinnacle Mountain.

And although W. J. Hardin had been dead these twenty-four years, his ghost still presided over the memories of old Nanito. That was the original name of Shingle Hollow back in 1884 when, at just sixteen, W. J. Hardin opened the store and post office there in the red mud crook of the road.

The keepers of W. J. Hardin's legacy were the live-in curators of the region's oldest continuously run family-operated country store. Hardin's was over a hundred years old and W. J.'s son, J. Lewis, was mighty proud of it. He and his wife, Ina, lived in a pine-shingled house that was cheek-to-jowl with the store; the two buildings were extensions of each other. The Hardins used the store as an extended living room and the shady storefront served as their front porch for social times.

The two buildings appeared inseparable as Siamese twins: the house didn't have a phone—the store did; the old house used to be the Nanito post office while the store served as community center and grocery-general-hardware-piecegoods store.

J. Lewis Hardin said he could see no plausible reason for ever changing the store one whit. It was a standing memorial to the figure they all remembered as the man who "did everything there was to do."

On wilting summer afternoons there was still no finer place in all of Shingle Hollow to sit out the heat, watch for folks passing on the Cove Road from Green Hill to Whitehouse, and share conversation.

The talk was of the present; about Eddie and Wanda Hill's robust boy, Ryan, there in the playpen. The great-grandson of the old shopkeeper—what a little bruiser he was, they all agreed. A young teenage girl rode up demurely on her bicycle, parked it, and affixed young Ryan on her blue-jeaned knee. The little boy's great uncle, Frank Arrowood, sang, "Whirly-gig, whirly-gig, whirly-gig—*whee!*" poking the squealing toddler in his ample belly.

Out on the gravel-floored, shady front, the sitters were assembled: Ina Hardin fanning herself with a *Biblical Recorder*, old Grover Robertson with his "go t'hell hat" and crooked walking stick, Wanda Hill, and Bland Waters. And also a vacant split-bottom chair contributed to the unshakable feeling that it was reserved for someone no longer there.

J. Lewis said of his father, "There wasn't a thing he couldn't figger. He could barber, pull teeth, depidy, he was fire marshal, game warden, deacon at Piney Knob Church, he delivered two'er three babies, blacksmithed, kept the store and post office for seventy years. Oh, did I say he farmed and sawmilled? Doctored too. That's right, he could do anything, bub.

"There wadn't no doctors y'know. He'd swab out folks' throats with blue-stone when the dip-theery was around. And I guess the only education he had was out of that Blueback speller. He holpt every grandyoung'un he had through high school." J. Lewis couldn't contain his pride for his father.

An occasional car shushed through Shingle Hollow's center, a singular business district composed of one store, the road to Piney Knob, no stoplight, and that hard right angle coming in from the Cove Road. You missed that curve and you wouldn't miss Hardin's store. "Two of 'em landed right where we're sittin' now," Ina Hardin said, grinning slowly. But back then it was dirt—or mud—and everything, not just vehicles, moved slower. The road was more like a character with its moods. When it was bad, it was awful. "I remember when the mud in that road would be thigh-deep." J. Lewis showed just where on his leg. And Ina said wryly, "That

The storefront provides shade for some summer fun.
Frank Arrowood teases little Ryan Hill.

road ain't a-been tarred that many years. Some people'd get stuck
up there on that hill and push and pull all day long."

As with all things of importance in Nanito, W. J. Hardin did
what he could about the road, scraping it with a mule-drawn sled
when the time was right. "Wagons did it all, weren't no cars a-tall,"
J. Lewis insisted. "To get stuff for the store we'd have to take the
wagon down to the depot at Gilkey and pick it up. Or buy herbs
from people 'round here and take 'em in the wagon and sell 'em in
Asheville."

The little store in Nanito (an Indian word of unknown origin,
pronounced *nanny*-toe) served a large hinterland in the days be-

fore good roads and automobiles. "Folks'd come here from all over." J. Lewis rattled off the names of communities, some all but nonexistent now: Otter Creek, Darlington, Piney Knob, Whitehouse, and Ayr.

The mail was delivered by old Oscar Geer riding on muleback from Darlington to Nanito with that mail sack slung over the mule's rump. The post office consisted of a window on the south side of the Hardin's house. You could still see where it had been, though it was cedar-shingled over now. Ina liked to laugh at the old house and call it "that old an-*tique.*"

The place changed its name somewhere along the way from Nanito to Shingle Hollow presumably because "everybody in the neighborhood had a shingle mill," J. Lewis said, demonstrating with his big hands how a shingle mill turned out machine-cut heart-pine "shakes" or shingles. It amounted to quite an improvement over the old hand method of splitting shakes from a block of wood using just a froe and maul.

Except for the stock on the shelves, Hardin's store looked much as it did in those days at the turn of the century: a healthy tomato vine was scaling one of the posts outside; around the other J. Lewis was growing something he called "angel's trumpet"; about two dozen squirrel tails hung decoratively on a wire between the two posts, attesting to the storekeeper's recent marksmanship. Inside the old store the simple pine floor was burnished by time; a wooden, hand-cranked phone hung on the wall; a bank of rounded glass cookie counters dominated one side. They were veined with cracks and splinted together with tape and bolts—bolts that had antique soft drink caps for washers. J. Lewis said with a grin, "Two li'l ol' boys was in here one night scufflin' and one of 'em stuck his head through that glass. I had to repair it myself. I was just a little thing, too, at the time. Run outa washers and went to using Coke caps." J. Lewis's more recent repair jobs on the cracked glass were effected with wooden washers, bearing the inscription: "Don't lay on me please. I been here a long time."

Items out of the past adorned the old store's walls. J. Lewis demonstrated how his father would "cut off a nickel or dime chew" with a chewing tobacco-cutter that looked like a finger guillotine. In its side the lettering read "RJR Tob. Co." and "Brown Mule." From the ceiling hung odd-looking contraptions and household items of which only J. Lewis knew the function. There was his mother's wooden mallet for "mashin' stuff up in them ol' black pots," a

J. Lewis is proud of his
homemade wind-machines
and the decorative squirrel tails.

wooden shoe-stretcher, plus something J. Lewis said was his dad's
bed-wrench, which had been passed down in the family for at
least two hundred years.

J. Lewis was equally proud of "mama's shuck mop," a curious
wooden-headed object with a long handle. "We didn't know nothing
about no *rag*-mop. Had to use corn shucks. Just stick 'em in these
holes and go to scrubbin' the floor till they wore out. Every family
used to have one. Reckon it's the last one in the county; all the
others been burnt up."

On the glass countertops, old decals advertising patent medicines
still hawked their wares. There was Ramon's Liver Pills for Head-
ache, Constipation and Biliousness, as well as Narcissa Waterman's
remedy for Scrofulous Eyes and Wild Hairs.

J. Lewis finished his circuit of the store at a long-legged, lead-
bottomed chair. "He'd just sit right up here and tend the store,"
J. Lewis patted the chair back respectfully. All this talk had set the
memories to rolling. "Remember the time ol' Oscar the mailman
rode his mule from Darlington to here—and forgot the mail sack?"
J. Lewis demanded of the porch-sitters. "Had to ride plumb back
to Gilkey on that mule to get the mail. My dad just died a-laughin'."

And it wasn't difficult to imagine the ghost of old W. J. himself,
sitting there rared back in his split-bottomed throne, holding his
sides with mirth at the thought of ol' man Geer having to ride that
mule plumb back to Gilkey for the mail sack.

Grover Robertson's Indian Fort

I know it was a fort. . . . Ain't no maybe about it.

Fat, heavy-bodied raindrops toppled out of the arching oaks like high divers, their random landings making for a lazy tattoo on the tin-roofed, three-sided shed below.

"*Whoop!*" A voice from within the shed's gloom shattered the pastoral calm of the Shingle Hollow woods. Materializing gradually like a vision, a figure presented itself from the darkness: an old man with a face restless with merriment, eyes that promised mischief, an educated brow, receding white hair that stood straight out on the sides like the fins of a '57 Chevy, and an uninhibited, gap-tooth grin. He wore a khaki shirt, loosely buttoned; baggy, patched jeans; and old brogans minus socks.

Grover Robertson cried out, in a voice full of gusto and exuberance, "Come to see the ol' Indian fort, have ye?" Some folks in Shingle Hollow might have regarded Grover as a hermit, but he thought of himself as just a slightly eccentric local historian-philosopher who preferred living alone and simply in his woodsy retreat.

Grover, eighty-eight, was at home there. The shed featured two woodstoves—one for heat and the other for cooking; a swaybacked couch sprinkled with pillows and old newspapers; a time-blackened oak floor punctuated with pots, pans, cans, and magazines; clothes on hangers festooning the bare rafters; doodads and gewgaws

Grover Robertson,
the self-appointed historian of Shingle Hollow,
leans through a window of the old log fort.

hanging from the walls—an out-of-date calendar, an American flag, kerosene lanterns, and newspaper clippings. The pungent tang of woodsmoke clung to the damp morning air under the dripping oaks.

Living in an open-faced shelter suited old Grover fine. He was tough and proud of it. Though when the winter got unbearable he might sit out a cold snap with friends and relations nearby, he scoffed at the elements most of the time. "Back when I was twenty-four I was a farm manager in Canada and milked fifteen cows before sun-up at fifty-two below zero."

He had been researching the history of an old Indian fort nearby in Piney Knob. But before he led the way over there, Grover sat down, rared back in his split-bottom chair, and verbally polished off his pet subjects, including the national debt, a Roman Catholic plot to take over the country, the wiles of French Canadian women, and the latest presidential gaffe.

People who knew Grover took the old orator with a grain of salt; and there was a good chance Grover didn't take himself too seriously either, for he was an incurable debater. His love for creative argumentation caused him to confess, "It's just one feller trying to get one word next to another to make some sech sense. And it's just for a rippit—and all sech stuff. A "rippit" was Grover's favorite term for a good time at a debate, like the times at Berea College in the twenties when Grover was a member of the debating society.

"Had a real rippit one time, invited all the girls and had refreshments, all such stuff, and Jim Johnson (he was a smart 'un) he took the re-buttal and I had the affirmative. Well, I's all shakey-lagged. Course, he didn't know that 'cause if he had, then he'd a-swamped me for shore. When it came my time I told him I's gonna cover my subject like that ol' American eagle—with one wing over South America and the other over Europe, and eating berries outa Jupiter!" Grover's eyes danced with the recollection of that triumph of words.

The old Indian fort was not far through the woods from Grover's place and Piney Knob Church—or, "the Knob church," as Grover called it. Clambering past a blasted mulberry tree to the rickety porch, Grover declared, "I know it was a fort—government fort. Ain't no maybe about it. As best as I can estimate, around 1812 when they was runnin' the Indians outa this part of the country."

The remains were a sixteen-by-twenty-foot silvery log cabin list-

"Wouldn't take much to fix it up,"
says Grover. "I *know* it was a fort."

ing to the starboard on its rock foundation on the low side of the
meadow. A rusted tin roof was partly blown off, and the elements
had done their worst in one corner. The center of the old heart-
pine floor and the sleepers beneath were disintegrated as if a piano
had been dropped right through the roof. Remnants of a chimney
were piled like a rock memorial.

Grover walked gingerly about the place, knowledgeably pointing to the remaining broad-timbered, whitewashed walls that were still solid and true and so expertly hewn that they lay only an inch apart "so arrows and sech couldn't get through," and to half-dovetail notches slanted "to keep the rain out."

The round, skinned, pine-pole rafters, tin roof, and window openings were new, according to Grover—"new" meaning after the government got through fighting Indians and when the place went to a succession of owners. Grover listed William Guffey first, a Mr. Smart, and then W. P. Patterson and his sister, and finally "Ol' man Jesse Scoggins who had it from 1836 to 1902."

Grover remembered the place from his boyhood. "Scoggins kept it the way it used to be. There was a chestnut log kitchen house, a log smokehouse and a log dormitory. Back in Indian-fightin' days, when there was something happening, then the soldier'd run up here from the dormitory to the fort. And there was an old cemetery up on the hill there." Grover eyed the pine-bristled ridge. "If you were a soldier here and you died, why they put you right here, that's all there was to it."

It was known as "The Old Scoggins Place," for "ol' man Scoggins," who Grover said was a "vet'inarian, tooth dentist, and a sergeant doctor. There warn't no hospitals in Rutherfordton, and this here place was a country hospital. We're standin' in the middle of it right now. And that ain't no lie," Grover nodded fiercely.

"It's owned now by ol' man Hyder down at IBM in Charlotte. They come up here on weekends and work on the place; keep it nice," he said. "Them government people might do something about making this a historical place. A few of 'em was over here a couple of days ago," Grover said with pleasure. "Wouldn't take much to fix it up." He went and sat by one of the windows beside the dry green mold on the gray walls and the English ivy persistently scaling the logs. "I recollect hearing tell of the story as a boy. They had some slaves over here a-plowin' and they looked across the fields—here come two Indians. Then, *spank*, and one Indian fell. And *spank*, the second one was down too," Grover held an imaginary musket cradled against his shoulder as he sighted down the invisible barrel. "Those two slaves come up to the man and said, 'Boss, we's scared; there's dead Indians out there,' and the boss said, 'Well, that's how they're supposed to be.'

"Those Indians prob'ly just passin' through," Grover resumed. "Didn't even know whites was here. But that was when folks were

Clambering around the fort, Grover speculates it dates back to "1812 when they was runnin' the Indians outa this part of the country."

runnin' 'em outa this country. I used to know where they were buried. Stones got knocked down. I put 'em back up once. But see, I'm gettin' old and that hist'ry stuff is gettin' gone . . ."

Away off across the meadow past the sagging log fort, a mourning dove set up hollering, "Who-*whoo*, whoo . . . whoo . . . whoo"—a plaintive elegy for fallen Indians and government soldiers alike whose unmarked graves dotted this peaceful woodland. Grover heaved a long sigh and straightened himself up, winking for emphasis, "Now that there's what you call chrone-*ology*."

UNION TRUST
FDIC

Tommy Robbins's Trolley Car Cleaners

There might be lots of people that thinks this is an eyesore. But . . . it's antique-ish.

Tommy Robbins loved those old trolley cars. Thinly disguised as a dry-cleaning establishment on a back street in Spindale, the two cars were the old man's pride and joy.

If Tommy closed his eyes and listened intently to the sound of the streetcar's sneezing, to the steam press shushing and the glass window's loose pink-plank, he could all but imagine Old 42 was in motion again.

He was eighty-five and liked to come station himself in a folding metal chair at the front of one of the twin cars like a motorman of old. Keeping his walking stick and pipe handy, Tommy stored in his corner a pack of pipe cleaners and an old Bible with its back worn completely off.

"You know, when I was a young man," Tommy put down his pipe, "I used to go to Asheville and ride this very same streetcar around town. Mr. Zeb Hensley from here in Spindale was the motorman for Old 42. I guess it was sort of a coincidence."

Back in the thirties Tommy was looking for somewhere in town to open his cleaning establishment. "But I couldn't find anything big enough," he said. "Well, I'd seen a streetcar that had been reworked and I thought that was the prettiest thing—so I heard they had them up in Hickory and I went up there. Well, they didn't have

Like a trolley car motorman of old,
Tommy Robbins sits at the head of the car.

any. So I went down to Greenville and they didn't either. Then I heard about this place outside Asheville that had streetcars from that city—and sure enough, this feller named Fortune had them. I bought two and hauled them down here."

For over thirty years Tommy ran his dry cleaners out of the two side-by-side silver streetcars. He'd retired the year before, selling the place to his cousin Dan Huskey, a retired country singer who shared Tommy's affection for trollies.

Dan speculated, "Yeah, there might be lots of people that think this is an eyesore. But there's others that say it's not." Smiling slightly beneath a trim mustache, Dan added, "It's antique-ish. I don't know, but I believe I'll just leave it the way it is. I mean, if it's gone, it's just gone. Streetcars—you don't find them around much anymore. It's good to keep a couple of memories, isn't it? *Sure* it is."

It about broke Tommy's heart to sell out. "Of all the things that hurt me the worst was knowing I had to get out from up there," Tommy said candidly. But at eighty-five, he conceded it was time to let a younger man take over. It was enough for Tommy now to visit daily, and resume his position at the front of Old 42. He was something of a fantasy motorman-emeritus.

Inside, the place was more like a streetcar than a dry cleaners. Like so many standing passengers, cleaned suits, dresses, and coats hung beside the windows. A fan in the rear clattered like rails clickety-clacking beneath wheels. The old, loose sliding windows rattled rhythmically as the steam press in the rear shook the car with its effort and chuffed clouds of steam.

At the front, with the window opened straight out, Dan welcomed customers—or passengers, depending on how you looked at it. Out front, the streetcars' headlights had been removed, but an imprint remained like a shut eye. The destination marker on the top of the car read "Dry Cleaning." The faded numerals of "42" could still be read in cracked gold paint.

Tommy never said it, but it was clear the Spindale lad had never lost his fascination with trolley cars. If he couldn't be a sure-enough motorman like Mr. Zeb Hensley, then at least he could buy him a couple of streetcars to run his cleaners in.

Now, on nice spring afternoons when he was feeling up to it, Tommy would take his place at the front of the coach, gazing down Davis Street. Perhaps he was imagining himself at the throttle, with Old 42 plying the rails, the windows clattering busily, the disembodied passengers of hanging clothes swaying with the trolley's

Tommy Robbins's trolley car cleaners wheezes and chuffs in another incarnation.

rhythm. The water pipes sang, the noisy fan clattered, clouds of steam billowed from the clothes press that chuff-chuffed above teams of flashing silver wheels . . .

Dogs would bark. Small boys in knickers would chase them down Davis Street, the trolley's solid brass headlights gleaming proudly. Motorman Robbins would change the placard from "Dry Cleaning" to "Main Street" and turn the fire-engine-red streetcar right out to the middle of town where ladies in long dresses and parasols and gentlemen in straw skimmers would be waiting to ride on Old 42.

Wouldn't that be a sight.

Winking and blinking,
the old carousel looks like a big birthday cake alight
in the early autumn evening.

W. C. Hathcock's Carousel

You won't see no prettier merry-go-round on the road.

Across the dusky hills the dinkle-donging music of the merry-go-round sounded like distant alpine cowbells. It was early September, and a light chill hinted of a quilted night after a shirt-sleeves day at the grounds of the Ellenboro school where the annual country fair was winking and blinking gaily.

The Colfax Free Fair was an autumn institution in Rutherford County: the staid WPA-era brick school hovering as a backdrop to the colored lights, music, and people at the fair on the softball diamond, and W. C. Hathcock's authentic carousel as the centerpiece.

That same enchanting machine had been coming to Ellenboro for the fair these forty-four years with Hathcock at the controls much of that time. Just as the carousel was the heart of the fair, W. C. embodied the soul of that most magical of machines.

W. C. was an avowed carny—more boy than man. His bright, childlike eyes happily watched the passing parade of wooden horses carrying "children of all ages." His wrinkled face seemed a contradiction juxtaposed to those boy's laughing eyes. Sitting in the center of the carousel with both hands on the metal control bar, W. C. said proudly, "The merry-go-round is fifty years old this April. I've been running it ever since I've been old enough—and before that I was riding it."

He pulled at the control lever, a pulley groaned, well-oiled gears meshed, and the whole spinning world increased its dancing tempo. "It ain't just because I work with this outfit, but you won't see no prettier merry-go-round on the road," W. C. announced.

The wooden horses were carved by four German brothers at the turn of the century, W. C. allowed. The children and parents of Ellenboro might never have suspected they were riding on priceless antiques. On the canopy above the riders, pastoral scenes had been painted. Carved wooden masks stared down at the garish carnival world whirling below.

It was a circular parade which W. C. professed never to grow tired of watching: a little girl wearing an "I love granddad" T-shirt was tearfully clutching the shirt's namesake. A mother held a tiny newborn atop a kind-eyed dappled mare. A gray-haired couple rode laughing for fully thirty minutes, smiling at each other in spite of themselves. W. C.'s white-haired, ruddy-faced assistant strode nimbly through the churning riders collecting tickets. On the horses, the child-riders were tirelessly happy, amazed and fascinated by the flashing colors, spinning platform, and the rinky-dink martial music from the old calliope.

The engine groaned like a complaining but faithful camel, and the carousel's organ played the twenties tunes and Sousa marches just as fast as it would go. "Only carousel with an organ like that that's still on the road," W. C. declared. It was a wonder to watch—air pumps and pulleys working the organ, a snare drum riveting its cadence, and a bass drum pounding ceaselessly. Inside the organ-works, wooden boxes shaped the often out-of-tune but endearingly sincere notes that poured out in an enthusiastic jumble. The music was like a Keystone Cop movie in which the film had been sped up and the notes all went scampering about wildly, waving their arms, bumping into each other, falling down, and jumping back up again.

The merry-go-round was a fine mix of engineering and flights of fancy. Huge beams, which had been painted year after year for each new carnival season, supported the central machinery. The fairyland of fantasy steeds took W. C. and any help he could muster six hours to set up. When they got it all done, and the sun set behind distant Hogback Mountain and the carousel lights came up, it looked as if some magical toadstool had sprouted in the old schoolyard.

W. C. Hathcock at the controls:
"I've been running it ever since I've been old enough—
and before that I was riding it."

In a fantasy world of flashing lights, music, and motion,
a young rider is transported to another world
on her prancing steed.

Just as proud as W. C., ticket-taker R. D. Freeman of Ellenboro said, "They's got two or three down in Raleigh. But this is far finer as you can see. I been to a lotta fairs, but this is the finest merry-go-round you'll find."

During a short break between rounds, a tow-headed blond girl mounted her horse, and after reassuring words from her dad, patted the wooden mane of her prancing charger. From the sidelines, on mortal ground, parents and grandparents waved and watched happily, staring transfixed at their offspring up there amid the lights, sounds, and flashing movement—maybe with some memories of their own.

W. C. at the controls saw it all, tapping his right foot to the rhythm, absently munching popcorn as he pulled the lever and the galloping calliope clattered to life again, now playing "Oh, What a Beautiful Morning." Like some galaxy, the starry merry-go-round began circling W. C. with a blaze of lights and music. The little blond girl on the dashing stallion was in a world all her own. And so was W. C.

GULF
GULF

Creed Wilkins's Acme
Service Station

They never figured gas'd go over forty cents a gallon . . .

Creed Wilkins's Acme Service Station was dying, but the old men pretended not to notice.

The sandy-colored brick Gulf station across from the courthouse square in Rutherfordton would soon be razed for a more cost-effective office complex, Creed's place being anything but cost-effective. It was—and had been for years—falling gently to its knees like Mr. Bojangles going down in slow motion.

Gulf wasn't spending any money on its older places, Creed said. He was looking to retirement soon, so when the time came, he figured he'd hang it up along with the Acme. He and his late brother had owned the place since the thirties, and very little about the Acme had changed since then.

At the Acme, time didn't pass; it crept. People only noticed its effects after many years of weathering and wearing. The peeling silver letters of "ACME SER. STA." marched in a semi-circle across a cracked front window so patched with silver duct tape that it looked like a map of Western Europe. The window wasn't there so much so you could see *in*, for it appeared seldom washed. Rather, its function was to allow light to fall softly on Creed's collection of citrus trees potted in halved oil drums on the ledge.

Outside the old Acme in Rutherfordton,
Creed Wilkins shows off a vehicle of another age.

Creed, a methodical man used to being free of the tyranny of time, was glad to talk about something as vital as his trees. The old men casually thumbing newspapers listened appreciatively from their sagging wicker chairs. "That lemon tree must be thirty years old. It was given to my mother by my brother-in-law. Now . . . she died in '52, so I know it's at least that old. She used to make pies off it." Creed reached out and plucked a sunny beauty the size of a small grapefruit.

"It blooms and bears year-round. About three or four times." He turned to another tree: "That's a miniature orange or kumquat tree. Sour-tasting though. It's just six years old. You can make marmalade outa this." The two trees crowded the front window, prickling the air of the office with a sweet citrus tang. In the warmer months the trees required direct sunlight, and Creed said, "We have to take them out front. Use a front-end loader—either that, or five good men to carry each one."

In the middle of the cozy office stood a kerosene stove, and Coke crates and slouching chairs orbited that glowing centerpiece on chilly fall mornings such as this. It was difficult to say, but the office appeared once to have been painted blue. Now, peeling paint hung from the high ceilings like draped tinsel, the ceiling boards sagging and bowing from the leaking roof.

In the garage where they changed oil and worked on an occasional car, the oily stuff spilled there over the decades had become so impacted with soil and grime that the floor's surface had a dark, cushiony character. A sagging men's room sign held up with a makeshift bit of spare wire also supported a rusting cowbell. It was anybody's guess why Creed needed a cowbell. Most likely it had just been hung there for some odd reason years ago—and like most everything else at the Acme, once in place, the old cowbell was never moved—and thus became a part of the whole, assuming a kind of subtle purpose like a piece of a collage.

Around the dim corner hung an autographed print of a presidential portrait. Behind dusty glass a bespeckled Woodrow Wilson, confident of his place in the history of the world and the Acme, stared benevolently down on the men's room.

The two rusting gas pumps out front registered only double digits. Caught thus in a time warp, they read 28.9 cents per gallon. It was a cruel reminder, and it made Creed shrug. "They never figured gas'd go over forty cents a gallon . . ."

Woodrow Wilson keeps benevolent watch
on the way to the men's room.

In one of the cool, dark stalls at the Acme, Creed kept a relic of local history: a dusty, once-elegant surrey sat back there like a mirage of wood and leather. Creed was proud of his surrey. "My sister and I bought this twenty years ago from the Coxe Plantation down at Green River, and we restored it." He let his eyes rove over the surrey while he swiped a ruddy face with one hand, roughly testing the day's beard stubble.

"We had to replace one tire—and liked to never found a man who could take and make a wheel like that with rubber on it. Found an old feller over in Newton. Prob'ly dead now." Instructing his men, Hubert and Silas, to help him roll the rig into the sunshine, Creed quipped, "Yup, that's the surrey with the fringe on top. That was in the big league class back then, just like a Fleetwood Cadillac today. A lot of buggies were to be seen, but most of them didn't have a fringe. I get a kick out of having it, and a lot of old people who come around enjoy seeing one again. A lot of young people have never seen anything like it except in the movies. We've not had it out on the road since an Easter parade here in town years ago. It's hard to find horses not afraid of cars," he said, as Hubert produced a cloth and started polishing the plush leather seats.

One of the Acme regulars approached the surrey. James Mathis was eager to tell his story. "I rode in that surrey when I was a little boy," he announced. "I'm seventy-one and I remember ol' man Colonel Coxe had that thing. I grew up out at the old Scott place just the other side of the Polk County line. Born and raised out there, went to the ol' Coxe school. I know that buggy's over seventy-five years old; more like a hundred."

Mr. Mathis went into high gear, "I can see it right now: be going long while I'd be walking. They'd pull up those two fine horses and I'd climb in. Yessiree, I'd ride right there," he pointed to the front seat. "Ride there standing on the floorboard. I guar-an-tee you I thought this buggy was a grey-aat big ol' thing."

The surrey stood self-consciously in the October sun, admired by the four men: Creed standing quietly off to the side under the sycamore tree, Hubert leaning nonchalantly on the top of a flame-orange Grand Prix, Silas with arms akimbo, listening repectfully to Mr. Mathis's memories.

"Yessiree, I recall the last time I ever saw this surrey out on the road. Charles Wilkins had it out in the Easter parade. He was wearing a great big top hat and driving a pair of big gray sorrels."

Always time for small talk at Creed's place.

Mr. Mathis sighed conclusively, "Yup, I been knowing that buggy for a long, long time."

When the surrey had been rolled back into its garage, the gentle pace of the old Acme resumed. Eulogizing the unseasonably warm fall day, Mr. Mathis strolled back into the citrus-sweet office. "Summer weather . . . summer weather," he soliloquized to anyone who would hear.

"Yeah, makes me wanna put in another bunch of cabbages and onions," responded Silas. Hubert, the body shop man, strolled purposefully but unhurriedly toward the shop, humming a rumbling baritone to himself, "Way down in Nooo Orleans . . ."

A woman customer stopped by for gas. Ringing the rusty pumps, Creed inquired sincerely, "How's your mother doing?"

"Gettin' along right smart," came the reply. And then their talk turned to layoffs and the slowing economy—talk that went far beyond the time it took to fill a gas tank.

An October breeze bathed the Acme with a pungent hint of woodsmoke, making the broad, dried leaves of the sycamore flutter fitfully like a church full of funeral home fans. Time, which didn't seem to exist at Creed's place, had finally caught up with the Acme.

Ayr

The haunted breeze whispered furiously through the listening pines above the last remnants of the forgotten village . . .

The late October wind moaned softly to itself over Ayr—as if the former tanners of that crumbled and abandoned village were flying through the trees, aching for the chance to be mortal again.

Beneath the Halloween breeze the ghost town settled imperceptibly into the Bills Creek hollow from where it had sprung a century before. There was not much left of the old tanning village of Ayr; nature moved too quickly to reclaim its own, reaching with eager limbs to enfold the weathered buildings and leaving only stone foundations as mocking headstones to yesterday's edifices and human travail.

Standing guard over that mystic cove near Lake Lure was a broad-umbrellaed, magnificent beech tree, its gnarled, gray, bulky trunk supporting a broad brush of colors: impossibly red-gold and yet yellow and still green, the canopy seemed to flaunt its hardy vitality over the death and decay that man's presence had left in this valley.

In stark contrast to the father beech stood the last upright building of old Ayr: dark and tall with foreboding windows staring out blindly, a door agape in a frozen wooden shriek. It was an old store with a steeply pitched tin roof now rusted into a dark russet crust

The last standing structure of the abandoned tannery ghost town slowly settles back to the earth.

teeming with honeysuckle. The chimney had fallen down and lay sprawled as if some giant hand had struck it dumb to the forest floor.

Holes in the roof permitted a teasing sun to weave weird and fantastic shadows on the weathered board-and-batten walls. Softly waving cobwebs curtained the windows. The haunted hollow was filled with the golden, trance-like haze of October and a foreboding silence.

Silence—except for the trickling dirge of a meandering spring just outside the old store, slithering through Ayr like a liquid serpent, and the selfsame song of rushing water coming from the other side of the overgrown pasture where Piney Creek hurled itself suicidally across worn rocks.

Silence. All quiet except for October's last crickets telling sibilant secrets to each other and a distant pair of chickadees chit-chatting in staccato arpeggios. Beside the sun-spotted stream an old buggy axle had been hammered deep into the pliant sand—to tie horses? For children of the tanners to play around? Questions like tortured wraiths raced invisibly through the haunted cove. What was this place? Why was the lovely village in the mountains abandoned?

Frank Logan, an old black man who lived back up on the main road at Bills Creek, had said the town was best known as "the ol' tannin' yard." It was the village that housed the tanners and their folks, and it was run by a man from Scotland named Reynolds. But the town had begun slipping away when Reynolds died. And when leather-processing became unprofitable, the place was deserted as people left for better jobs. "I ain't been down there for forty or fifty years," Frank said.

The late Clarence Griffin, Rutherford County historian, speculated that the tannery operation was started in the town of Rutherfordton by the Grangers prior to the Civil War. During the war the Confederate government took over the place for the production of cavalry saddles. After the war the tannery grew so quickly that the Grangers realized that an experienced tannery manager was needed, and a Scotsman named Frank Reynolds who was skilled in the trade was named supervisor. It was unclear just when the tannery was moved ten miles west of Rutherfordton up to the secluded folds of the mountains, but it must have been effected to take advantage of space, proximity to logging operations, and

A broad-girthed beech tree stands guard over
the decaying ghost town.

water power. Supervisor Reynolds named the town Ayr, after his
Scottish birthplace.

The historian noted that fine leathers were made there, and
were shipped all over the East Coast. The fall began when "tan
bark" grew scarce. Some speculate that the demise of the American chestnut in the great blight was part of the reason for the
tannery's decline. The chestnut, called "acid-wood" by the moun-
taineers, was a rich source of tannic acid. Reynolds died in Rutherfordton in 1918 at the age of sixty-nine, and the little tanning
village died with him.

Of the tannery building, all that remained was the rock foundation rearing its massive mossy head above the forest floor. The other buildings had collapsed in fatigue, but their remnants were still visible. Scattered about the valley were other hints of Ayr's past. In a depression, bracken-clothed bricks lay in a tumble of what might have been a molasses mill. A rusted, denim-blue coffee pot pouted emptily beneath a leafy blanket. Doors of the old store displayed rusted, ancient locks ineptly trying to keep out time's rotting ravages.

Maybe the old store had also housed Ayr's post office. Now only hardy holly, blazing hearts-a-bustin', violet asters, and green-sheathed rhododendron posted their marks along the cryptic path that served as a sunken rural route to the ghost town.

So the gentle October breeze rustled uneasily. Withered leaves like perished tanners wafted slowly back to the earth. Ayr's last remaining building appeared to be settling by the minute back into its buckling foundation in the abandoned hollow where the mountains of Bills Creek fold and crumple like a crazy quilt. The haunted breeze whispered furiously through the listening pines above the last remnants of the forgotten village of Ayr.

Part Six   How to . . .

This makes the third generation of Padgetts. We still hold to the old ways—and I want to learn 'em how to kill hogs. The day might come when they'll need to know.

—Walt Padgett

Seventy-year-old Joe Clark Frashier collects cane
for mashing prior to cooking the squeezings into molasses.

Joe Clark Frashier and Molasses Making

Joe Clark Frashier was worried. "My fourteen young'uns didn't know how to make 'em," the abbreviated third-person plural pronoun being Joe's affectionate way of addressing the sweet subject of his concern: molasses.

"I thought I better show my kids how—before I left," the seventy-year-old clan chief said one golden September morning. It was the long-awaited molasses-makin' day in the Harris community of Rutherford County, and Joe and his "young'uns"—all grown and married now—were ready to have at it.

It had been twenty-seven years since Joe had put a hot pine fire to a pan of cane squeezings, but the know-how all came back. "Hit's like drivin' a car," the lanky, overall'd farmer explained. "Once't you've done hit, you'll never forget."

Joe and his brood had been planning for this day since last spring—planting, caring for, and harvesting the cane by hand. But even more tedious was the process of building the molasses mill pretty much from scratch. He and his boys put together a molasses shed with a custom-built stove, chimney, and long, multi-channeled cooking pan. His other boys had scouted around for a used molasses mill to grind the cane. They finally found one that was about a hundred years old—"down below Ellenboro," Joe said. "It was *old*. They quit makin' them way back 'ere. Wasn't nothin' but the *arn* part. We had to build and mount it on a base and connect a stout pole to turn the mill." He had wanted to do it the old way—by one-horse power—but that hadn't worked out, and Joe elected to turn the "'lasses mill" with a slowly circling tractor.

It was the first day of September, a morning as crisp as a ginger snap. The operation began slowly, but Joe and company sensed the momentum and anticipation; all were in high spririts. Joe's son Glyn, wearing gloves and a battered Korean War Air Force cap, fed the fresh-cut cane into the iron jaws as Don Epley drove the slowly circling tractor. His wife Wilma stoutly pitchforked mashed cane remains out of the way. Joe's wife Demmie sat beneath a tree with a gaggle of "grandyoung'uns." She had broken her leg just a couple of days before. Joe, firing up the stove, was good-humored about Demmie's fall. "When I told her I'd be countin' on her to help me work the 'lasses pan, she went right home and fell out the back door," he said with a laugh.

Joe's fire was ignited in a burst with a fatty pine knot, and he perched on a homemade stool to watch the green liquid simmer and steam until it came to a frothy boil. His daughters—Judy Epley, Joyce Jones, Jean Hopper, Brenda Jackson, and Margaret McComb—were on duty with everything from spatulas to hearth shovels, skimming the green goop off the surface and depositing it in a nearby "slop-hole" dug in the ground.

The boiling green juice was in a rolling turmoil, having entered the molasses pan a khaki color, and then turning golden by the time it reached Joe at the far end of the cooking process. "Whoo-eee! That smells good!" Wilma exclaimed as a sweet, wet mist enveloped the downwind skimmers and scrapers. The oven got to roaring, and the woodsmoke and steam fumed out of the little open-sided shed. The brick chimney top turned dark as a howitzer barrel, blackened from blasting the sky with sweetness.

The anticipation grew as thick as the sweet fog billowing from the golden bubbling pan and the tangy woodfire. Old man Joe Frashier was everywhere at once: scooping juice that was boiling too quickly to a cooler position along the cooking pan, finding a new handle for a skimming ladle, making sure there was enough fresh cane juice in the burlap-covered barrel. And he was having a grand time of it.

While Glyn Frashier feeds cane into the grinding gears, Pantha Epley pours freshly squeezed cane juice through the burlap strainer and Cindy Jones stirs.

Holding up his ladle, Joe expertly eyed the golden globules that clustered lazily along the overturned lip. Everybody in the shed was watching this final testing; it was like Christmas morning and Papa Frashier was slowly opening the door to the living room full of surprises. "Now . . . it's gettin' purty," said Wilma, breaking the spell.

"Lookin' like syrup now," Judy chimed in.

"Them's gonna be purty, ain't they?" Don said admiringly.

In answer, Joe pulled the plug at the "done side" of the cooking pan, and the scalding molasses came gushing in a brunette waterfall into a cheesecloth-covered pail below.

Then Joe took a spoonful and let it cool, offering it to the waiting grandyoung'uns. Pam Hopper was the first to try, with Demmie administering the first taste. The little girl leaned forward tentatively and took the spoon to her mouth—the whole operation ceased as everyone watched this momentous occasion. The little girl screwed her face tightly in a grimace as if she had been force-fed a vile castor oil. Everybody broke into laughter and Demmie exclaimed, "Why, I think she's never tasted hit before!"

The freeze frame came unstuck: the Frashier family pitched back into their work with the molasses coming hot and heavy now. There must have been a dozen workers all busy in some phase of mashing, loading, pouring, pitchforking, stirring, ladling, or straining the stuff.

Folks were running back and forth tending to the boiling juice. Wilma took a turn on the tractor that turned the mill. The air was redolent with the sweet pungency of cooking cane. Toddlers with Grandma played beneath the oak tree. A shapeless old dog deposited itself under her chair. And Joe, proud as a country monarch, manned the final stage of the cooking molasses beside a long wooden table now groaning with the cooling jars of amber sweetness.

The big country family was laughing and joking—enjoying each other and the unforgettable event. It had been like a present from old Joe.

Walt Padgett and Hog Killing

We still hold to the old ways—and I want to learn 'em how to kill hogs.

When the weather turned bitter cold after Thanksgiving rolled past—and when the late November moon went to wasting—that meant just one thing to the Walt Padgett clan of McDowell County: hog-killing time.

Walt arose at four that morning to begin preparations for the late autumn ritual. Son Joe was right-hand man, and the services of expert hog butcher Frank Tate were indispensable. Before daybreak Walt and Joe had the fire going out between the meathouse and the hog pen. Frank arrived, grumbling good-naturedly about not getting through his first sip of coffee before Walt had called him out.

The two corn-fed pigs were shot, and they wallowed in the muck of the pen, making an awful mess. The men had to get ankle-deep in goo to get the dead beasts out of the pen so they could scald off the hair with boiling water.

Walt, who was nearing sixty, insisted hog butchering was a folk art; you don't just go at it without knowing what you're doing. Frank, there, was something of a community expert on the subject, having done already upward to fifteen hogs that season. "The way people worry me to death—un-*huh!*" Frank shook his head in mock complaint.

Under the supervision of Frank Tate,
Padgett boys scrape the hog.

It was a skill handed down from father to son. Frank learned it from his father, Ab Tate, who in turn was taught by his father, Henry Tate. Walt's father, Dan Padgett, "learned me—and he was the first man in these parts to sugar-cure his," Walt said as a gaggle of grandchildren clustered around, helping him and ogling the hog, or giggling with pretended horror.

The sights of a hog butchering may strike the uninitiated as gory and carnal. But Joe saw it differently. "It might look bad now—but it'll sure taste good on the table."

Walt was determined to pass on the fine art of hog butchering. "This makes the third generation of Padgetts," he said, waving a well-worn boning knife in the direction of the five youngsters nearby. "We still hold to the old ways—and I want to learn 'em how to kill hogs. . . . The day might come when they'll need to know."

Walt saw the annual ritual as a ceremony of the horn of plenty, a celebration of a full meathouse. The event was a neighborhood affair, and a festive air—as redolent as the robust smells of the operation—permeated the place.

Two forty-gallon drums of scalding water sat on a bed of coals emitting clouds of steam. Hog's hair and mud made a cold muck underfoot. Though everybody's feet were muddy and their hands crimson with the business, the fire cheered them, and laughter filled the chilling air.

"We use everything but the squeal," chuckled Joe Padgett. "Yessir, everything but the squeal—and we'd use that if we could find a use for it."

On a broad hardwood chopping block Walt worked with an eroded double-bladed ax. Strung up against a stout, double-trunked poplar, the gutted carcass hung to drain. Two heads hung by their snouts on the side of the meathouse. "Ooooh!" The two girls, Tina and Amy, wrinkled their noses and acted as if they thought it was disgusting.

The young boys, Chris Lonon, David Padgett, and Bo Lonon, bravely did their carving, helped Walt, carried buckets of water, toted meat to the house, and stoked the fire.

On a carving board set up on two sawbucks, Joe was working with "the recipe." It was Grandpa Padgett's own sugar-cure formula: a tangy-smelling powder of red and black pepper, brown

Walt Padgett checks as son Joe and boys
prepare meat using "the recipe,"
a time-tested family formula.

sugar, and salt. Each piece of carved meat was rolled in the mixture, wrapped in brown paper, and put in a sack, which was tied and hung up. Walt said it would take about fifty days "for the meat to take the salt."

"The old people say if you kill your meat in November you won't lose any of it," he said. "We usually do it on Thanksgiving or the day after—on a day when I'm not working and the kids are out of school and can watch and help. The weather was bad this morning, but we got a head start and now it's clearing off."

The skies had indeed cleared obligingly, allowing sun shafts to ply their way down through the steep woods to the Padgett homesite in the creek cove. But along with the clearing came the hint of a cold snap. Out of the cloud-blustery blue sky, snowflakes flurried down. Frank, working in shirtsleeves, called out to one of the boys, "I believe if you bring my jacket I might put it on."

As Walt dropped pigs' feet in a bucket, he instructed, "Saves money too, raising and killing your own hog. We fix it up just like we want to. Fatback for cooking, tenderloins, backbone, sausage, livermush from the head and liver. We render lard out of the fat and use that for cracklin' bread . . ." That prompted Frank to interrupt spontaneously, "And it's dee*lish*-us."

Walt and Frank both contended that the moon had everything to do with proper meat at hog-killing time. "When the moon's going away the least, that's the time to do it. If you kill your hog when the moon's wastin', then it'll cook in the pan right. Otherwise, it'll just swell up in the pan if you don't. That's old folks' saying. But that's how we do it," Walt advised.

Just then, Walt's wife, Edith, came out of the house carrying a plate of tenderloin biscuits, followed by red-haired Amy with a fresh pot of coffee. "We're goin' to cookin' 'em before we've even finished cuttin' 'em up!" grinned Walt with relish over a savory, fresh-cooked meat biscuit.

Edith, feeling the cold, installed a toboggan cap securely over her head, lamenting in a sad but proud tone, "It's a mean time," for she'd spend the rest of that day grinding sausage and taking care of her end of the job, which was to put up the meat. Standing closer to the fire, she observed with a keen weather eye to the west, "It's as cold as a frog."

The operation in full swing, where they use "everything but the squeal."

The Padgetts weren't selfish with the kill either. "With six children and fourteen grandchildren, by the time you give 'em all a mess around—there's not much left," Edith observed. By midmorning the work was done—with Frank hollering, "That's hit!" and Walt echoing, "That's all she wrote!"—with satisfaction over another year's hog butchering well done.

Bertha Byrd and
Apple-Butter Making

That's the best eatin' there ever was . . .

James Byrd's students claimed he had "apple butteritis." When his cousins over in Relief went to making their annual run of apple butter, the Burnsville high school librarian said he just had to be there.

"I could smell that sweet apple butter cooking away across the Toe River as I came in," he told his cousin Jewell Warrick, who was hustling around taking directions from her mother, the old master, seventy-year-old Bertha (but everyone called her "Berthy") Byrd.

It was one of those spanking-clear, bright November mornings; a perfect day for the family's autumn ritual. Sixteen-year-old Leisa was helping her grandmother, whose advice, "Ripe apples make the best apple butter," had always been followed religiously. "An' you might just as well take the whole day to make a good batch of apple butter," Berthy added. Her husband Charlie, eighty, had started peeling the native stamen and delicious apples the night before, and the cooking had started at eight that morning.

Jim and Jewell Warrick had set the fire between the two barns and the farmhouse. A ten-gallon kettle mounted in a cast-iron tripod squatted twelve inches over the flames. The smell was a delicious mix of nose-wrinkling woodsmoke and sweet apples cooking. Saffron leaves clung to the sugar maples beside the fading red barn.

"Berthy" Byrd keeps the apple butter stirred,
while Jewell Warrick stokes the hardwood fire.

"Slow cooking—that's the secret," said Berthy, sitting in a ladder-back straight chair by the locust and oak fire. "Got to be a brass kettle," she instructed. "This one was Charlie's mother's. His mom and his dad always done this. I been making apple butter since I was ten years old; that makes sixty years of apple-butter making."

Berthy was dressed for work: an ankle-length, green print dress, a light sweater thrown around her shoulders and an old-fashioned mob cap covering her gray hair. She rocked back and forth in her chair, stirring the red goo with a five-foot-long paddle; the thing looked like a child's hobbyhorse. "If you don't stir, hit'll burn," Berthy said. "Zebulon Hartley made this paddle out of poplar. I wore out three or four in my time." Berthy leaned forward, scowling into the brew. "Jewell, there's an apple seed in it."

Plucking the errant apple seed from the mixture with a fire-blackened wooden spoon, Jewell recited the family recipe: for a ten-gallon batch they used five bushels of apples and five pounds of sugar per bushel. "You cook up the apples for one hour or more before you go to adding sugar," she said. But the major ingredients for apple butter were patience and elbow grease. They kept the pot at a low, rolling boil for about five hours—with the deep crimson stuff blooping out of the pot occasionally like a sweet-smelling volcano.

Jewell, helping Charlie out of the house and into a folding chair in the sun, noted, "It hops when it's cooking." And Berthy agreed, "Oh, you couldn't make it without some of it a-jumpin' *out*."

Berthy said she didn't know where the custom of cooking apples came from. "All I know is that they've been making it ever since I can remember. Apples are so plentiful around these mountains. You got to do something with them: cook 'em for applesauce, dry 'em so you can be eatin' on 'em all winter, and three-layer fruit-cake—why, I just love that best of all."

James explained, "When they say fruit in this part of the country, that means apples, not anything else."

Another year of apple-butter making got Bertha to thinking about old times. The thirteenth of fifteen children, she was raised simply. "When I was comin' up we didn't have none of this modern stuff, but we were so happy. There'd be times when neighbors'd go sit and talk of a night, help shuck corn, snap beans, piece quilts, and make molasses.

"My mother made her apple butter with winter-john apples and sweeten hit with molasses instead of sugar—and oh Law', hit would make the apple butter turn just as dark red as could be. Then they'd put it in crocks with paraffin wax over the top and keep it in the springhouse.

"Hit's really cookin' down now, yes it is," Berthy rocked in her chair methodically. "When we go to the fair at Burnsville and make apple butter (been a-makin' it for eight years on the square), people ask me how I stand it stirring all day long. Why Law', it doesn't bother me—I been doin' it so long.

"When I tell people I'm from Relief, they always want to know how come it's called that. It's because John Peterson had a store back then that carried this patent medicine called Hart's Relief. People used it for everything and bought so much of it, when they needed some more, they'd send the kids to the store and tell 'em, 'Go down and get me some relief.'" Berthy said the store was gone now, and so was the medicine—all that remained was the name: Relief.

Yellow jackets divebombed the red and gold apple peelings in a cardboard box. Jewell added more apples and sugar. A fall breeze brushed the yellow maple leaves. Bertha let Jewell spell her on the stirring. "Leisa, chuck that fire up a little bit," she said. The talk turned to the weather. Berthy remembered "the May freshet of 1900," and nobody could forget the devastating 1977 flood in Yancey County. "The Elk Shoals church steeple was found plumb down in Greenville, Tennessee," Berthy said mournfully.

Jewell nodded, "Now, that's getting to be a pretty color." James added that when it rained hard in Yancey County, "You can feel it, there's still a fear in people. If the 1977 flood had come during a school day, it would have been a panic. We were lucky."

"They claim we're going to have the hardest winter ever," Berthy offered. "But I just take it a day at a time." Then: "Oh Law', Jewell, I believe it's a-ready."

Taking a tin fruit-strainer, Jewell placed it on top of a quart mason jar and began dipping the apple butter out of the kettle with a long-handled tin cup, adding a capful of cinnamon oil to the jar. "It'll sure warm you," she smiled prettily.

"It takes a lot of work," conceded Berthy. "But that's the best eatin' there ever was . . . and when you take a wooden spoon and

reach down and sop out what's left in there on the sides of the
kettle, why Law'!" she exclaimed. "It's worth it for that first bite of
apple butter on a hot buttered biscuit—un-*hunh*."

Because they couldn't wait to test the run, Jewell and Leisa had
prepared for this moment with a batch of biscuits. Passing them
around, they daubed open biscuits with apple butter from the
wooden spoon.

James licked his lips in appreciation, "This tastes like nothing
you can buy in the supermarket. But apple-butter making like this
is a dying art; it's really something out of the past."

Part Seven

After All These Years . . .

I don't complain. I've had the good with the bad. Losing my son during the war was almost more than a body can take. But I don't complain about my life—I've had good children, and good grandchildren—and even good great-grandchildren.

—Aunt Lena Dellinger

Ask not what your
country can do for you—
ask what you can do for
your country.   John F. Kennedy

Aunt Lena "Nannie" Dellinger, Matriarch

It was always my plight to keep boarders.

A world of ice had transformed the apple orchard outside Lena Dellinger's kitchen into a glittering crystal palace. Beautiful but treacherous, the ice storm had snapped power lines, leaving many folks in Avery County on that Thanksgiving Day without electricity—no power for lighting or heating the holiday houses, no electricity for cooking the turkey.

Somehow Aunt Lena's place in Crossnore had been spared—which was a good thing because the ninety-year-old mountain matriarch had a full house that day.

The chestnut bark–covered house on the hill was the holiday haven for the Dellinger clan that congregated at "Nannie's" especially for holidays. A gang of twenty was not unusual at Thanksgiving and Christmas—with kin driving in from as far away as Jacksonville or Atlanta, and one of four daughters flying from Tokyo.

As a light snow began frosting the groping elbows of the apple trees, the kids in snow boots clumped in and out of the breakfast room—tossing coats and hats toward doorknobs and washing-machine tops with scant attention to aim. The family gathered in that breakfast room because it was Aunt Lena's headquarters, or rather her throne room—for she reigned over her consider-

Aunt Lena Dellinger making an Afghan out of granny-squares:
"I don't complain about my life. . . .
I've had good children . . ."

able brood with a gentle mix of affection and direction. Laughing heartily, she refused to chide muddy-booted grandchildren. "I'm not much of a dirt-chaser. Never said I was. But they keep coming back."

The breakfast room was practically all windows, like some many-eyed Argus poking its head out into the wintry orchard. When the mountain weather was milder, the breakfast room became a little greenhouse, a sun-splashed sanctuary for Aunt Lena's troupe of African violets, begonias, and Christmas cacti that mustered in orderly ranks on window shelves.

The kitchen table represented her headquarters and was not so much a place for eating as it was an open filing cabinet where a typical montage would include a cut flower, a worn leather-backed Bible, copies of *National Geographic* and *State* magazines, current newspapers, mounds of correspondence, her stationery and pens, coffee fixings, a half-eaten pound cake, a jar of her famous home-made wild raspberry jam, and her ever-present phone. Overhead, a set of glass wind chimes plinked a comforting melody—stirred by the updraft of a space heater at Aunt Lena's side. Beneath the table an aging red dog groaned with rheumatism. The walls were sunshine yellow, further contributing to the sense of good cheer, warmth, and nurturing in this little mountain winter observatory.

She sat in a wooden armchair beneath a hand-stitched sampler bearing former President Kennedy's famous quote: "Ask not what your country can do for you—ask what you can do for your country." Immediately beneath the Kennedy sampler hung a framed, typed message from then-President Truman notifying Lena and Theron Dellinger of the death of their only son, W. C., in World War Two: "W. C. Dellinger stands in a long line of patriots who gave the ultimate sacrifice for freedom. And that as long as Freedom lives, he lives also . . ."

W. C.'s death had brought her low. But the old mountain woman was made of stern stuff. "I don't complain," she said over the cereal boxes and African violets. "I've had the good with the bad. Losing my son during the war was almost more than a body can take. But I don't complain about my life—I've had good children, and good grandchildren—and even good great-grandchildren." Now, she was piecing together another Afghan coverlet for some lucky grand-child. The woolen blanket of brightly colored "granny-squares" was for yet another generation.

Some of the older members of the family crowded around the oval table, and nursing coffee and pound cake, they had encouraged Aunt Lena to tell the old stories. The grown-ups knew them by heart but needed to hear them again; the younger people were eager to hear the telling for the first time. Aunt Lena was ninety; there might not be another Thanksgiving like this ever again.

She was born in 1890 near Mooresville to a family that believed in education. Her older sisters, Annie and Eunice, went to Flora McDonald College. Lena recalled, "Then it came my time, and after two years there, I looked at my old parents and how they were worrying themselves to death sending us to school. So I just decided to stop—and I went to substitute teaching."

At nineteen she married Andrew Crowell and followed him to Richmond where he enrolled in the Presbyterian seminary. "It was always my plight to keep boarders. Well, it was natural for me to cook. We took in four boys with bad stomachs; they couldn't eat the cafeteria food. But I fixed 'em up—and at the same time made enough to keep us a-goin'. Then we moved to the delta country in Mississippi where Mr. Crowell had his first congregation. I didn't like it," said the outspoken old woman. "Meanest people you ever saw. And I don't know, I didn't like being a preacher's wife. I was a Christian, but it's such a public thing. Everybody in the congregation is watching you to see what you're gonna do next," she said with a laugh. "You know they do that, don't you?"

They had their first child and moved to their second parish in Kentucky where Mr. Crowell died of rheumatic fever. Lena was in a tight spot, a young widow with a four-year-old to support and take care of. She came back home where good fortune awaited. Her sister-in-law, Mary Martin Sloop, needed her to cook for her husband, Dr. Eustice Sloop, the famed mountain doctor of Crossnore. They called him "Uncle Doctor" in the family.

"Mrs. Sloop was anxious for him to get good food. She was so busy and he would neglect himself if not cared for," Lena recalled. She began by working several summers to see if the arrangement would work. Her introduction to Crossnore was inauspicious. The train trip from Mooresville required two changes, one in Statesville and another in Marion. The train only went up the mountain as far as Ashford in North Cove. In 1915 the remaining twelve miles of switchbacks scaling Linville Mountain had to be covered by horse and wagon.

A man named Uncle Gilmer met her at Ashford. She recollected "how mountainy" he looked: white handlebar mustache, plaid flannel shirt buttoned to the neck, gray dress trousers, and red suspenders. It was a cold March day, and Lena said she wore "three coats all at once and Uncle Gilmer just sat there in his shirtsleeves. I had little Annie Laurie wrapped in coats too. Some family down in the cove there had heated soapstones and we put them at our feet, and Uncle Gilmer didn't put on a coat till we got to the top of the mountain."

When they got to Crossnore four hours later, Lena asked Uncle Gilmer, "Well, where's Crossnore?" Uncle Gilmer just shrugged—"there wasn't anything to see." She went to cooking for the Sloops and caring for their two children. She recalled being "mortified to death" because Mrs. Sloop insisted that she put "six eggs in one batch of biscuits—that was her way of making sure that Uncle Doctor got his nutrition."

She was offered a teaching job in Mooresville if she would "get some more schooling," she said. "So during the summers in Crossnore I had to go to summer school at Boone. So how did I get there? By horseback! It was the summer after the terrible flood of 1916 and the river was all over the place. There wasn't no road. It took nearly all day to ride the twenty-two miles. Ol' Joe Williams rode with me carrying Annie Laurie for I wouldn't go without her. Then when we got there, he rode back with the animals." Lena attended Appalachian Training School for Teachers for six weeks.

It was that summer that she met a mountain man named Theron Dellinger. The local storekeeper took a shine to her, and Lena said they courted for a couple of years, as was the tradition. They even waited an extra year to get married because the flu was rampant in the country. "We thought we were dodging it—but coming back from Mooresville after getting married, we both got it and liked to have died." The newlyweds were put to bed at "Gran'pa Dellinger's place under the hill," where they were nursed back to health over the course of several weeks.

While they were recuperating Grandma Dellinger heard that Nin Vance was willing to sell off fourteen acres right in the middle of Crossnore—a wooded hillside with a small house. Lena recalled with relish, "We bought this land while we were in bed."

It wasn't long after that transaction that they learned Nin was retiring as postmaster, and Theron had the idea that Lena could get the job because of her background as a schoolteacher. "I took the exam at the courthouse in Marion," she said, "but I couldn't hardly think for a band was a-marchin' up and down the street. Bang-bang-bang, up and down." She laughed. "And I only had a certain amount of time in which to take the test, for the train was to leave for Ashford just a certain time. I guess I passed, for I got the job." She took the train back to Ashford, and again rode a horse twelve miles back up the mountain to Crossnore.

"They put me in as postmaster. Theron helped me. I taught school and had a baby every few days, and so on," she said with a laugh. In 1927 the Dellingers decided to build a new house. Her sister Bertha saw a picture in the newspaper with a design and plan that pleased Lena. They picked the site and went to work. "The studding, as Theron called it, came from the big pines from Uncle Arthur's land sold to the government for the Linville Falls picnic ground. We decided to put chestnut bark on the sides, and when it wore out, put weatherboarding over that—but as you can see—it never wore out. Mr. Wise and his uncle built it for sixty cents an hour. Both of 'em wonderful carpenters. Never put in a nail they didn't need. I always say: there wasn't a piece of lumber that I didn't tell 'em where to put. But I overdid it. Put in too many windows. Thirty-seven of 'em. That's too many."

Lena and Theron had four girls and a boy of their own. But there were four other children Lena had a hand in raising. Two boys who needed a home found it under Lena's protective wing, as did a grandson raised as one of their own, and an Italian Jewish refugee from Mussolini's fascist regime.

"Mrs. Sloop came to me one day and said, 'Lena, I want you to take Jack, and I think you can help him.'" Lena related how Jack Hame had escaped from Italy with his family across France and taken a boat to the United States where the family was denied entry because they were Jewish. They went to Cuba for a time until young Jack could get into the country and be taken care of at the DAR school at Crossnore.

But the short dark Italian who couldn't speak English was having trouble getting along with the other boys. Aunt Lena took Jack in and for three years raised him as one of her own, until his parents could gain entry to the United States, find work, and send for Jack.

Although forty years had passed, Jack, who had become a successful New York City businessman, had never forgotten his mountain mama. "He still makes a big sputter over me," Lena said with pleasure.

"Back then when me and Theron had the movie theater, the boys used to work the place for Theron. Jack learned how to run the picture shows when none of the others could. That just shows how progressive he was. And on the way home, W. C., Richard, and Billy'd stop at the café and get a hamburger. But Jack'd just say that he'd get a cold biscuit off the kitchen table at home. So he saved his money—now he's gots gobs o' money. I guess he's a millionaire. And he always gives me all the credit, but Law', I don't know why."

Jack Hame wasn't the only child of the mountains who still doted on the nannie. The holiday crowds just seemed to grow each year at the old chestnut bark house when the snow flew about the gnarled apple trees.

Aunt Lena, finally retiring after a full day, took to her bed, sharing that space with her companion, Millie, a bug-eyed, black, roly-poly terrier that adored her. "Dogs are just dogs—no way you're going to make them a person," Lena offered.

The room had a poster with a motto that might well have been her credo: "The greatest truths are the simplest." And also in that room Lena kept five clocks going all at once—and all showing different times. "That's just my tickers," said the old woman with a wink, "so I know the world's still a-goin'."

At Lena's birthday party, a great-granddaughter
provides a second wind.

Saney McEntire, Oldest World War One Vet

I'm liable to take off any minute now.

Saney McEntire, ninety-three, claimed to be America's oldest living veteran of World War One.

The old soldier's legendary status was accepted among the McEntire clan of Piney Knob and Shingle Hollow in Rutherford County. But the fact of the matter was hard to prove—not that this bothered Saney at all.

"Yep, got a letter from somewhere saying I was the oldest livin' veteran of World War One. . . . Yeah, oldest in the *country*." But Saney couldn't remember where he put that letter, and the Veterans Administration's files showed no record of such correspondence.

The rub apparently came from Saney telling a little fib about his age when he enlisted in the U.S. Army in 1916. He was afraid he was too old, and so Saney claimed to have been born in 1888, making him twenty-eight. But according to family records, he was really born two years earlier, in 1886, which would correspond to the age he now claimed to be—ninety-three.

It seemed all very complicated to the old man, and he didn't really care about the distinction that much. He lived a simple life with his nephew Virgil in a modest frame house that Saney had

Saney McEntire, ninety-three,
takes his ease in the morning light:
"I'm too tired to live."

left only twice in two years—and then only to go to the mailbox. His memory was growing opaque when he tried to talk about his past, slumped in his favorite armchair with his shoes off. His discharge papers helped jog the painful recollections of hard times in the service of his country.

Saney went to Columbia, South Carolina, to enlist, and after being accepted as young enough to serve, was sent to Camp Jackson, and then on to France. His nephew pointed out, "Back then they rushed the boys right into the war without much training. Their tents, sleeping gear, and rations must have been awful. I remember how bad the K rations were in World War Two, and that was thirty years later. You could only eat the stuff so long."

Apparently war life was too much for the textile worker from Rutherford County. Saney said, "I fell off from 220 down to ninety pounds." His outfit was camped somewhere in Luxembourg, and he remembered "a bummed-out town with nothin' left but a church or two." He was interested in seeing the sights, and one day while walking round, an Army doctor spotted him and realized Saney was wasting away.

"There was something the matter with me—but they didn't know what it was. But *I* know what it was," the old man confided, leaning close. "It was piles and arthy-ritus."

Saney's discharge papers were not much help at clearing up the record. A doctor's handwriting described Private McEntire's condition as "resulting from physical strain from work, drill, deprivation, sleeping on the ground and lack of proper food."

Saney was sent back to a field hospital in Bree, Belgium, for four weeks of rest. By the time he had recovered enough to be released, he found that his old unit had been sent to Germany. "I was told it would be impossible to rejoin my old outfit—so they sent me home," he said.

For a year and a half Saney was so weak and gaunt that he couldn't hold a job—no matter how hard he tried. Saney said it took him years to regain his health and weight. Finally he got back to a relatively healthy 180 pounds and went back to work in the mill. Some years later he opened and ran McEntire's Store, a one-room country grocery and gas station on Piney Knob Road, which later became the Pick Shack, a bluegrass watering-hole run by Saney's great-nephew, Dennis McEntire.

He retired to live with Virgil just up the hill from his old store, surrounded by kin and memories. Typically he spent his days watching his color television with the green tint turned up full—a habit relatives affectionately called "Saney-vision."

But at ninety-three—or was it ninety-one?—Saney declared that his fight was about finished. "I'm too tired to live," he said, reciting a litany of troubles that seemed to soothe him. "It makes me weak just to eat. I can't be here much longer. Why, I'm liable to take off any minute now."

But Virgil and the facts said otherwise. The McEntire clan was renowned for their longevity. Grandparents living well over the hundred mark were commonplace. And there was Virgil—who doted on Saney with "country foods, fresh stuff outa the garden, and three oranges wringed out fresh every mornin'."

The old veteran piped up, "Ain't got me as married, d'ya? 'Cause I'm not no married man. I got to wait till I get old enough." And then the faintest tremor of a smile. "'Cause I lack twenty years yet of bein' old enough to marry."

John Wesley McCall, 100-Year-Old Farmer

Had to give up farming last year. Got too trembly.

When John Wesley McCall turned 100, practically the whole community of Glenwood turned out to salute the community patriarch. "Didn't think I'd live that long," said the old farmer and storekeeper.

His son Wayne had told the gathering at the Glenwood Methodist Church, "His wealth today is not so much measured in material goods but in love and devotion to his family, the inspiration and example of his life, and the admiration and respect for all who knew him. His life is a fulfillment of Proverbs 22:1—'A good name is rather to be chosen than great riches.'"

The week before the big party, John had taken the opportunity to sit out on the back porch and recollect his lifetime. It was one of those golden October mornings when the sourwoods had gone to hearty burgundy, and the distant flaming poplars marching up the flank of Huntsville Mountain looked like a regiment of yellow-topped candles. John leaned on his cane and squinted out across the valley. Falling acorns noisily peppered the roof of the wellhouse nearby. Distant crows yammered over the wheat fields. Fall crickets wheezed in the yellowing grass around John's old house.

He was born the oldest son and third child to Isaac and Virginia McCall in a log house in Paddy's Creek, a community that was

From his sunny back porch,
John McCall gazes out at his fields in Glenwood
and recalls old times.

later submerged by Lake James. He remembered the log cabin heated by just one fireplace and lighted by kerosene lamps. When he wasn't helping his father on the farm, John attended school. "For three months out of the year we went to school; it was a log house too. Walked a mile and a half to get there. Had about twenty-five students—all ages in one room with one teacher. I went till I was about twenty-three," John said.

At that age, in 1903, John moved to the North Cove community at the base of towering Linville Mountain. There he opened a store. "Went into the mercantile business," he said. McCall's General Store carried everything from patent medicines to horse shoes. In 1913 he married Mary Alaska Lonon, known to all as Alaska. John explained, "I think somebody'd been to Alaska and back about the time she was born. That's how come she got that name."

John and Alaska were living in the back of the store when on the night of July 16, 1916, the big flood washed much of North Cove down to the Catawba at Marion. "Hit was an awful time," John said shaking his head. "Hit commenced a-rainin' about five and poured the rain till about two or three in the night. It worried me right smart. I walked the floor all night. Why no, Alaska wasn't scared so much; she went right to bed and slept the night through.

"The water came right up to the front of the store—dug out a hole in front of the store house. Hit washed away my hog. And when I looked in the pen, there was somebody else's hog in my pen. It'd washed another hog down from higher up the cove I reckon.

"That was an awful night. I finally went off to sleep after the rain stopped. A crowd woke me up. About three folks got killed up there. That water never did get in the store, but it just run down the road in a big sluice. The railroad washed away too. Took about a month before they ever run a train through there again."

John decided to leave storekeeping and take up farming in 1920. He bought his 350-acre farm in Glenwood. For sixty years he farmed and logged. John said with sincerity, "Had to give up farming last year. I got too trembly." But he still had a firm enough grip to swing an old mowing scythe and keep the woodshed stocked with a battered ax.

In their time, John and Alaska brought up seven children, losing one preschool age boy to disease, and educating the rest. "Put all six through college, we did," he says. "Hard work it took, too. Took a lotta farmin'. But I wanted 'em to be as well educated as other people—and there was a good many going to college then."

A well-stocked woodshed
attests to John's axmanship.

John raised enough corn, chickens, cattle, hogs, and wheat so that during the Depression "we were all right." Raising and educating six children was an accomplishment he and Alaska (who had died two years previously) never took lightly. They joined the Glenwood Methodist church where for over sixty years John was a respected leader and teacher. His son Wayne was fond of recalling, "It wasn't so much 'Shall we go to church today?' as much as it was 'We don't want to be late.'"

John loved to farm, plowing with a team of horses, or hauling loads of wood to Marion five miles away for four dollars a cord. "I could get two trips to town a day. Two or three hours a trip," he said, as in the background the shushing, windy sound of automotive traffic from the modern highway punctuated the old man's memories. "No, the young folks of today they don't understand the way it used to be. You don't see horses and wagons and such. Used to be a store at every crossroads and a blacksmith shop. . . . But they're all about gone."

Julia Brown and Lucy Gray, Missionary and Nurse

Two of the awful-est old women *you ever did see!*

The two bent old women stood on either side of a tree scarcely taller than themselves. It was November, and the little oak had only a half-dozen dried leaves left—even so, one of the ladies was beating on the branches with a cane while the other was picking up each leaf as it fell and methodically depositing it in a basket.

It was the sort of vignette that typified Lucy Gray and Julia Brown of Rutherfordton. The two widowed sisters, both in their eighties, lived together in a neat little brick house in the middle of a perfectly manicured yard that lay on the sunny side of the old residential hillside overlooking the town below.

The two old sisters complemented each other so well that they were like two sides of a single personality. They had lived together so long that when they spoke they completed thoughts and sentences for each other.

Julia, the older and larger at eighty-four, was physically the boss and made of stern stuff. A retired head nurse with the well-earned nicknamed of "Big Abe," she had been known to scoop up deposits from neighborhood dogs found in her yard and march across to the offending owner's porch—there to leave it with a kind

The two old sisters of Rutherfordton:
Lucy Gray, left, and Julia Brown.

but firm warning and a peace offering of pound cake. With one neighbor who owned a Saint Bernard she developed a special relationship. Julia considered herself something of a neighborhood appearance monitor and upon at least one occasion had taken her clippers to a neighbor's gangly hedge.

Lucy, the younger at eighty-two, was deferential, and it seemed her mission to be always smoothing things over for Julia with her sweet nature and forgiving ways.

After beating the hapless oak leafless, the two sisters waded through their garden picking beans. Then they retired to the kitchen where Lucy cut up celery and took an occasional noisy bite from a stalk.

They were born at the Abrams homeplace of Sandy Springs near Coxe's Crossroads on the edge of Polk County. Julia could recall when their new log cabin home was built in 1895; she was three years old then. "It was just one big house. One room," Julia said. "All the neighbors came to help build it. Uncle Bill Gray, he built the chimney and it's still standing. Built it just out of rock and mud. And the neighbors would come in and help put the house up. Its big logs are still standing. Now the joists—Granddaddy Abrams hewed those, and you won't know when you see them that they weren't sawed. And he hewed them with a broad ax." Julia said.

"He was a genius," Lucy concluded.

Julia again: "The only heat we had was the fireplace. We cooked in the fireplace too. Then they got busy and built a log kitchen just a little ways off from the house and a breezeway between 'em. We boiled all our washing at the spring with two big washpots. Boiled and rinsed 'em," Julia said.

"Rinsed 'em five times," Lucy amended.

"Well, we rinsed our clothes, I'll tell you that," Julia continued. "We had what we called a paddling bench with a paddle and when we washed 'em a little, we'd put 'em on that bench and paddle 'em and that helped to get the dirt out. Then we'd put 'em in a pot and boil 'em. And we used lye soap Mother made out of the ash hopper. Boiled down the ashes to make lye."

Julia started school in a one-room log structure called Solomon's Temple. Julia recalled, "It had a big fireplace and one log taken out for a window. Our benches were trees cut down and split open and pegs put under the rounded part for legs. We got water at the spring, and we had to go to the spring to wash our slates and get our drinking water. Where that school stood used to be a little bush—now it's a big ol' oak tree. And the steps went right up by it and the little tree was right there. And there was one little ol' boy there, and when I started up the steps he was standing there with his little ol' nasty nose and he grabbed me and kissed me as I came by—and I slapped him!" Julia broke into an embarrassed chuckle.

By the time Lucy got to school two years later, Solomon's Temple had been rebuilt and covered with "planks," and desks had replaced the crude log benches. Lucy remembered at recess they played with something called a Flying Jenny. She described it: "You take a stout sapling and cut if off about waist-high. Then you take a little sapling and split it and put it on the post. Then you can push it around and around and around. That's a Flying Jenny. That's the only thing we had to play with."

Discipline was hard to keep with "fifty children—a good big crowd," Julia said. She remembered most vividly the time their log bench split apart "with me 'n' Bob on it. Everybody else laughed—and then the teacher made me 'n' Bob stay in from playing to punish us. Everybody laughed but we had to stay in because we were the ones who fell down."

Julia went through the ninth grade at a seminary in Saluda taught by "Northern teachers." Lucy went on to nearby Hillcrest High School in Landrum. She finished there in 1916 and decided she wanted to do something useful with her life. Lucy recounted how "I spent three weeks praying. I'd slip away from my folks and I had a place over in the woods I went to pray three times a day. I'd come in to dinner and then go back, come in at supper and go over again afterward. Julia didn't even know about that," Lucy conceded shyly. "I'm a great believer in prayer. I prayed that the Lord would lead me into something that I could be useful in the lives of other people. At the end of three weeks I got a letter from Miss Carrie Johnson who was one of my school teachers asking me if I would consider coming into mountain missionary work.

"Well, I could have just shouted," Lucy smiled. "I said, 'My prayers are answered.' But Dad was pretty particular with us. He wanted us raised right. I asked Mother about it first, and she said, 'I think it'll be fine.' So Dad was plowin' in the field, and I made an excuse to go carry him some water. That was my time to ask him.

Well, I stood there chompin' and chompin', twistin' and turnin'. Then right to me he says, 'Well, what do you think about your work in the mountains?'

"I said, 'Dad, I think I'll go if it's all right with you.'

"'Oh,' he says, 'I think that's the very thing.'

"And then I lit out. Took the Tweetsie to Roan Mountain community. I never saw a more needy place, or a more lovable people. I stayed there fourteen years," she concluded happily.

Julia catalogued her life financially. "I recall the first quarter I ever had. I was five years old," she began. "My daddy gave my brother a gun cap and didn't think it was any good. He put it on a rock and hit it—and I was standing there over it when it fired and flew into my forehead. It stayed there awhile and when I was ready for school it kinda had swelled up—but ol' Doc Twitty (y'know John Twitty, it was his granddaddy) was out there in the country to see a man. and he come by and took his pocketknife and cut that piece of cap out of me. And when he got through my daddy asked him how much he owed him and Doc said a quarter. And he said I was such a good patient that I deserved the quarter— so he gave it to me. I took that quarter and bought me a slate, a pencil, and a writing tablet, so I was ready to go to school. And I still had some money left; now that was my first money," she declared.

"Then when I was about eleven or twelve, I made my next money picking cotton. It was thirty cents a hundred pounds, and I couldn't pick a hundred pounds in a day to save my life.

"I was eighteen when I made my next money. I went over to Tryon and took care of an elderly woman. I stayed with her about eight months until she died. Then in 1919, September the first, I entered nurses' training at Rutherfordton hospital. They paid me eight dollars a month. I worked three years and got my diploma. My first money from that was taking care of Dr. Washburn's mother. Then I came to the Alexanders in Forest City and took care of the family, a governess sort of. They had a little baby. That was Little Jakie—that's the one runnin' for governor now y'know— and I stayed there until he was fourteen.

"The hospitals back then weren't equipped to handle births so as a part of our nurses training, we had to take midwifery up.

Julia takes a break from her hoeing chores to accept
a glass of iced tea from Lucy.

Dr. Biggs and I birthed twins over yonder on the Mill Hill one time—and another time we saved a baby, I remember: the mother had had a hard time and was dying. The baby was born but I could see it was dying too. Hadn't breathed yet. Well, the doctor was busy saving the mother, so I took that baby and dipped it first in a pan of warm water and then into a pan of cold water. Well, that baby came alive just like that. That baby's a grown woman now. Don't recall her name, and I don't know if she knows that story at all."

Julia went to the Elkin hospital in 1938 where she was a nurse for thirty years. In 1940 she married Mr. Brown. Her face crackled with laughter, "Go on, put it there—I was forty-five. He had six children—and we lived happily ever after."

Lucy had also married a widower in Roan Mountain, a Mr. Gray. Julia grinned, "We both took leftovers."

But Lucy responded defiantly, "Well, I wasn't ashamed of mine nor you of yours!"

When both their husbands died and their parents passed on, too, Lucy recalled, "I asked Julia if it wasn't time for us to move back a little closer to our homefolks." They built their house in Rutherfordton and moved in "on the fourteenth of November, 1967," Julia recited precisely.

Mrs. Brown and Mrs. Gray (known affectionately because of their married names as "the colored sisters") made their lawn and garden a showplace. The lawn was mowed by barefooted Julia "to keep me from slippin'," and their garden was "thick as hair on a dog's back," Julia declared—with all sorts of vegetables. They filled their days with tending to yard, garden, and each other—as well as their neighbors.

Their favorite story they loved to tell on themselves concerned their moving back to Rutherfordton. Julia and Lucy both laughed when Julia repeated it again: "When we first moved down here, all my old friends that got up old like I was wanted to give us something to go in the yard. Well, I couldn't get anybody to dig any holes or anything, so I just—we just planted it ourselves. Everything that's planted out there Lucy and me did it—except that tree right there and those two big oak trees. Well, this old lady nearby said to a cousin of mine, 'Have you seen those two old women who's moved in on Meridian Street?'

"My cousin said, 'No! Why, who are they?' Well, she knew who we were perfectly well, she was just going along to see what the other'd say.

"The lady says, she says, 'I don't know. But it's two of the *awfulest old women* you ever did see!' Said, 'That ol' big 'un she's a-diggin' the holes and that li'l'un's a-carryin' the water!'"

Lucy concluded brightly, "We were putting out our shade trees to please us. You know, when you look out there at these trees and plants and all we've done to this place, you know it's something to be proud of."

Charlie Harrison Lance, Horse-and-Buggy Mailman

The mail had *to go through.*

Charlie Lance could see it all just as plain as yesterday.

From 1915 to 1952 he carried the mail in the Cane Creek section of Buncombe County by horseback, horse and carriage, and finally Model T. The rest home he lived in used to be a cornfield that was his bypass around "the biggest mud hole you ever nearly saw." The fine irony of that juxtaposition was not lost on Charlie's lucid mind.

Ninety-two years old and blind, Charlie folded his hands across his stomach, his sightless eyes bright with his memories. "I can just imagine how it was. Y'see, where this building is sitting was a cornfield, and I'd just drive around up here to get around that ol' mud hole," he said.

Charlie was born in 1893 to a sharecropping family in the Fletcher community south of Asheville. His parents sensed the boy was destined for better things and named him Charles Harrison Lance for former President Benjamin Harrison, who had just lost his reelection bid against Grover Cleveland. But the nickname that took was "Judge," and Charlie told it like this: "About the time I was just walkin', my daddy saw me a-toddlin' around, all short and stubby like ol' Judge C. M. Pace down in Henderson-ville, and he said, 'Well, there goes the Judge,' and the name stuck with me. My people call me that to this day."

Little Charlie did well in school, and he was particularly good at figures. His studying was done in the most Lincolnesque of situations. "I'd just lay flat on m'belly in front of the fire and let the reflection of the fire light up my book. Y'see, that and ol' kerosene lamps was all we had all my school days. You couldn't imagine anything like that now, could you?"

Charlie became a bookkeeper and considered himself lucky to not be a farmer. "When I was growing up that was about the only thing a boy could do—farm." His father talked him into taking a civil service test to become a rural route carrier for the post office. "I stood the exam and was one of the lucky ones," Charlie said.

But after his first day on the job Charlie didn't feel so fortunate. It was an eight-hour, twenty-two-mile trek by horse-drawn carriage through the mud. Charlie still remembered vividly that first day in 1915. "I was so disgusted. It was the first day of February and cold. I said, 'I can make a whole lot easier living than I can in this mud!' But my daddy insisted I stay with it."

Charlie would set out from the Fletcher post office about 8:15 every morning driving his one-seated buggy drawn by a single, dependable horse like Frank, his last horse before the conversion to automobile in 1927. Charlie sat on a padded buckboard with the mail safely stowed in a leather pouch at his feet. A wide, round, heavy canvas umbrella was his only protection from the elements. "It helped some, but it didn't keep me dry in a good rain," he said. "And in the summer it kept me cool."

When Charlie carried the mail, the postal service's motto that vowed "neither wind, nor cold, nor hail, nor sleet, nor dead of night can stay the postman from his appointed rounds," really meant something. From his chair in the rest home the old mail carrier declared stoutly, "The mail *had* to go through. Good night, back then they didn't know what paved was! I laughed and told 'em I didn't have but one mud hole and that was *all the way.* Twenty-two miles. Nothing but one mud hole to another, start to finish."

Next to the mud, it was the cold that bothered Charlie the most. "I guess the roughest I've seen in winter was the times when ice'd freeze right on the lines of the bridle of the horse. I just had to bundle up real good. Before I set out I'd heat a brick on the woodstove at Fletcher and wrap it with paper and put that at my feet.

That would help part of the day; but from then on, it was just tough; that's all there was to it.

"My wife Mary, she'd put a piece of meat between a biscuit, and by lunchtime it'd be frozen. Y'know it was rough times."

But Charlie always knew how important his job was. "I was the only way of people communicatin'. That was before the time of telephones, or electricity and TV and radio; the mail was all there was. Lotsa times I'd be the only person people out there saw of a day.

"Oh yeah, coming down a long straight stretch I could look down the road and see maybe half a dozen people standin' by their mailboxes waiting for me to come along. The women they'd be out there with their rag rugs they'd make on home looms. Mostly people sent letters to relatives and to mail-order places like Sears and Montgomery Ward, because they didn't go to town much—except to list and pay taxes—or when court was goin' on. They'd go mostly for observation, if they wasn't being tried themselves," Charlie said with a laugh. "No, folks didn't go to the city every day. It's not the way it is now. What you didn't raise you done without."

From his buggy, Charlie operated what amounted to "a rolling post office—that's what it was," he said. "I could do about everything a post office could: take money order receipts, sell stamps (two cents a letter and a penny for a postcard) and mail packages of all kinds.

"In the spring o' the year a lotta farmers ordered chickens from hatcheries. They'd come in crates, hundred to a box, all peeping along. I'd get used to the noise. Sometimes I'd have so many I'd have to tie 'em on the back of the buggy.

"I remember the most unusual thing I tried to deliver. I had one lady who had a son with a girlfriend down in South Carolina. He wanted to send her a present, so he caught him a li'l ol' 'possum and fixed it up really nice. Well, I couldn't accept it; that was against regulations. That lady she got real indignant. It *was* packaged up real nice in its cage," Charlie said, shaking his head.

The big flood of the summer of 1916 disrupted mail service, and Charlie's people "lost all connection with the outside world," he recalled. "We didn't have much mail to deliver for about three or four weeks because the flood washed away the railroad from Asheville south. Yeah, that was bad times. Right after the flood, when mail started again, the roads was so bad filled with mud, the only way I could get in there was to deliver the mail on horseback; you couldn't get around by horse and buggy.

"The flood washed away several bridges across the Cane Creek, except at the Alexander place. Ol' Mr. Alexander he saw that bridge was settin' to go and he chained it to a tree so it wouldn't go down." When conditions improved slightly, Charlie resumed delivery with the horse and buggy but remembered that "some of the bridges were knocked sort of sideways so I'd have to get down and unhitch the horse, lead him across, and then pull the buggy across the bridge myself." In other places where the bridge was out, "if the stream wasn't too large, you'd just have to drive the horse across—ford it, y'know.

"Yeah, you's out there on your own. If something broke, then you just had to make do. One time I's driving along and my horse fell down and broke the shaft from the wagon. I fixed it with an ol' oak limb I found. Bound it with the leather mail straps."

Charlie became something of a leading citizen along the banks of the Cane. "People on the route seemed to think I could do anything. One ol' feller had been foxhunting and stopped me by the mailbox. 'I want you to come look at my hound. I think he's been snakebit,' he said. I told him to just keep 'im in the dry and he'd be all right—and he was.

"Then there was this ol' woman with a big ol' butcher knife waitin' for me once. Said, 'I think my cow's got holler-horn.' What that was I never did know. The superstition was that if you took the cow's tail and split it with a knife, it'd cure it. She wanted me to split her old cow's tail, but I told her, 'Looky here, I'm not a veterinarian. I'm just your mail carrier.'

"And quite often a farmer might want to know what to do for a horse with spavin on the leg. That's a swellin' in the joints. An' I'd tell 'em my cure: trade 'em," Charlie said with a grin.

About 1927, the post office converted to automobiles. "I don't suppose there's a horse-drawn route in the country anymore," Charlie speculated. The switch from horse to horsepower didn't solve all of Charlie's problems. The mud holes along the Cane Creek Road were still formidable obstacles. "I'd have quite a bit of trouble with axles breaking," he said. "I chugged into the biggest kinda mud hole and broke the king pin on my front axle. Well, I looked around and there was a stackpole for packing fod-

der, hay, and such, around. I run it under the front axle and got
the car out. Then I noticed this wheelbarrow in a farmyard nearby
with an axle about the same size. I asked the farmer if I could
borrow that wheelbarrow axle if I'd bring it back the next day. He
said yes, and I dismantled that wheelbarrow and dropped it in
there just as happy as you please. It just exactly fit the king pin for
the Model T.

In 1952, after thirty-seven years of running the muddy roads
along Route Two in Fletcher, Charlie retired. At the time he quit,
he was still driving that Model T. And of those twenty-two miles,
his route had only one mile of pavement. "Blacktop like you have
now—they didn't know what that was," he said.

The changes had been profound along Cane Creek. Where the
stream and road ran into what Charlie still called the "Charlotte
highway" (US 64–74), developers had discovered Fairview, and it
was quickly becoming a preferred bedroom community for Asheville. The old mail carrier had a thought or two about that. "I hear
they got a bank and a drugstore and I don't know what-all. Yeah,
Fairview's got *growing pains.*"

Out Charlie's rest home window, down across the neatly mown
grass where "ol' man Alexander's cornpatch" once stood, the Cane
Creek Road hadn't seen a mud hole in many a year. "Yeah, it's a
nice blacktop now," Charlie sighed. "The fact about the matter—
there's not many roads that aren't blacktopped if they're used at
all," he said in wonder.

Where Charlie once fought the axle-deep mud holes with Frank
the red sorrel straining at the bit, the Cane Creek Road ran hard,
black, and impervious with asphalt. Homesteads offered mailboxes along the twisting mountain road like memorial markers to
the old mail carrier. Homes, some of them populated by sons and
daughters of Charlie's old customers, sprouted television satellite
dishes like gargantuan toadstools in the yards.

"I'd like to have one of those satellite dishes," Charlie vowed, "if
they just didn't cost so much. Yeah, I'm nearly blind, but I study
the TV. Like the old feller says—I do pretty well for the shape
I'm in."

PARKS HILL STAMP WKS.
RUBBER Stamps

Ernest Edwards, Photographer

I was one of them old-time picture men.

The old photographer Ernest Edwards himself made a picture: in the second-story window of the wistfully green, tumbledown house, the drawn face of the old man was framed as he sat there watching the traffic on the road from Marion to Rutherfordton. Then when viewed from inside, Ernest resembled paintings from the Flemish period, illuminated by soft window light.

One leg was folded over the other; on the uppermost knee a soiled green cap perched. Underneath his brown suit a pair of decrepit suspenders hung limply, their resilience being of another day. A many-holed black leather belt seemed to hold the eighty-three-year-old retired photographer together. Ernest's large hands were tool-like, tanned and smooth from use. He had the face of a "perticular man," riven with wrinkles. What he was lacking in molars he more than made up for with hair; he possessed a full shock of white brush that showed no inclinations of receding.

"I was one of them old-time picture men," Ernest declared, pale-blue bachelor's-button eyes snapping proudly. "I guess I could make any type of picture a man could want."

Ernest got into photography at thirteen after he had dropped out of grammar school in Greenville, South Carolina. Picture-taking and especially the darkroom work fascinated him. "The

Framed by his window high above the road to Rutherfordton,
the retired photographer Ernest Edwards watches the world go by.

way I got into it was because of cure-osity. I was just a boy and had
to do it all on my own," he said, recalling the days of 1913 when he
couldn't just go out to the camera store and buy premixed chemicals that dissolve instantly in water. "I had to do it all by trial and
error," he said. "I went to the druggist and asked him what I
needed. He said some of this and some of that. I bought a one-
pound package of that sodium sulfide—but the pictures didn't
come out. I went back to the druggist and asked him how come?
And he said, 'Well, I guess you need to add some more chemicals.'
So I added sodium carbide, potassium bromide, and gen-u-wine
metol—and I think it was sodium hydrochloride—and it began
to work! Then for my fixing bath I used 128 ounces of water with
one and a half ounces of sodium sulfide, acetic acid, and boric
acid." Old Ernest recited the formula for various mixing baths as
easily as a country cook relating the time-tested recipe for scratch
biscuits.

"I never had no courses nor nothin'. I spent two years practicing
before I ever went to picture-taking for anybody else." In 1915
Ernest went into business for himself as an itinerant photographer.
He had a darkroom set up in his father's house in Greenville, and
he'd get himself a driver, "throw my cameras in the back seat, and
take off."

He grinned broadly. "I been to might near every town in South
Caro-liney. Carried my background with me; a big paper roll, one
black and one white. Took pictures of families, individuals, buildings—and when I wudn't doing that, I'd do views . . . landscapes,
don'tcha know."

He refused to drive himself even though he owned a Model T.
"I'm a little bit perticular. When you've got a whole lot on your
mind you ought not to be driving. Why, my mind's been busy ever
since 1913!" Ernest laughed as he said it. Then growing serious,
he cautioned, "But you gotta be perticular about chemicals,
though. Some of 'em's poison y'know."

In his time, film was four to six cents a roll, and Ernest charged
fifty cents for an eight-by-ten-inch, black-and-white photograph.
"I liked a camera with a cloth that I can throw over my head
and see what you're getting. By golly, I don't like these Polaroid
cameras—they do all the darkroom work for you. Takes the fun
outa it." Ernest preferred the large format, view camera mounted
on a wooden tripod, the kind of camera he used to photograph

Old eyes: the sightless remains
of Ernest's camera.

World War One army camps. "Not long after I got hooked up with picture-taking, I got to photograph some of that war. Took lots of pictures of soldiers at camps around Camp Sevier and Columby. Yeah, then I'd go back to the darkroom in Greenville and make those pictures."

He worked before the days of flashbulbs and strobe lights, and so when there wasn't enough light to take pictures, Ernest used explosive flash powder. He would pile a mound of the silvery powder on a plate, open the camera's shutter, and then ignite the powder with electric wires. The blinding flash would produce enough light to expose the negative. Ernest said he ordered his flash powder from out of town, and made it explode by "taking two wires and touching them to make a spark in the powder, and that would set it off. But you had to be real careful with it. You could get yourself burnt if you weren't careful."

Ernest also improvised with his darkroom equipment the way

he did making his own developer and fixing bath. "Made my own enlarger. Used the lens out of an old camera, and rigged a light in a stovepipe for the top. I made might near all the pictures I did outa that enlarger. Made me a printing easel frame outa wood, too."

In the forties he moved to the mountains of North Carolina where he worked in the textile mills and as a baker. The chemicals he had been mixing by hand all those years had started to bother him. He said regretfully, "I quit picture-taking on account of the chemicals was about to get to me."

When his health began to fail and one of his ears started hurting him, Ernest elected to "go to a holiness church and see what I could do about it. Wellsir, I went in there and the man asked if anybody out there was a-hurtin'. Well, my left ear was giving me a time. I couldn't sleep, couldn't eat, couldn't think. So I went on down there and those people come up and got me on the floor and rolled me around. Holy rollers, I guess you'd call 'em. But any-how, they rolled me around till that eardrum busted—and from that day I've never heard outa that ear. But it's not hurt anymore eithers, so I guess the Lord he's got a perticular mysterious way of working."

After recovering from a pair of heart attacks, he opened a rub-ber stamp business at home. "It's just a-something to be a-doin' something," he said. Ernest spent his days in a worn, long-ago-gold easy chair, dabbling with the rubber stamp machine and watching the traffic. "I like living here on this corner by the highway for I see all the cars that come along. I never seen the likes of it. Seems like there's more cars since they went up on gas," Ernest said, scratching a white-stubbled chin thoughtfully.

"If I was to tell a young person what to do about going into the picture business, the first thing I'd learn 'em would be: don't be in no big rushing hurry, and study it out beforehand. Picture work is one of the greatest things we got I reckon."

Easing himself gingerly out of the sagging chair by the window, he went over to his bed, and from beneath it he pulled a cardboard box. He rummaged through it; then finding what he wanted, re-turned in his measured pace. It was a handful of his old pictures. He looked proudly at them: photographs of mills, mountains, church congregations, and families standing stiffly for the old photographer's hooded glass to wink their images into eternity. Ernest looked up and announced with a mischievous grin, "I might go back into that picture work sometime."

E. B. Hyder: "What do you think about that?
Didn't write my first song till I was eighty-seven years old."

E. B. Hyder, Songwriting Nurseryman

I wrote me a song . . .

E. B. Hyder, eighty-eight, was alone that Christmas for the first time. His wife had died the year before. But to keep him company, the old nurseryman of Rutherford County had his memories—and his new song.

"Do you know I wrote me a song?" his eyes fairly crackled. "What do you think about that? Didn't write my first song till I was eighty-seven years old."

E. B. sat in his sunny little front room where he had propped a tiny Christmas tree that was all but weighed down and obscured by wires and colored lights. It was a young balsam he was growing in his Green Hill nursery—just as he had been growing things and planting trees all over Rutherford County for the last sixty years.

"My daughter she rid me around Forest City last fall. Boy! It was a sight to look at them trees, all colored red and orange and just as big and round as you please. Never reckoned I'd live to see them trees to grow to be so big."

But trees weren't the only thing that E. B. had been growing; as his wife lay dying, a thought began germinating in the old man's mind. And just before his wife died last January, E. B. put it all together.

"I decided I'd write me a song, even though nobody never heard me sing a-tall. Well, I don't know where the song came from, but I was troubled about my wife. I just got it in my head I'd make me a song. I started by putting the words together—y'know, just the way I wanted 'em. Then I went to hummin' it . . . and then I went to singin' it—and then I put it all together.

"Then I took the song to my wife; just lyin' in the bed there—she didn't say nothin'. I just sang it to her. She put her hand on mine . . . and smiled. That was just before she passed on," E. B. said simply.

"Now, nobody can't sing it but me," he said, brightening. "It's wrote *right*. D'y' wanna' hear it?" Sitting straight-backed in the modest brick house "I built my own lone self," E. B. perched on the edge of his chair, and fixed his eyes on the scene out the window where his junipers and shrubs climbed the hill to the highway. E. B. sang with a strong, old farmer's voice unadorned by string or chord—his plaintive, rough voice lilting and swooping like a hawk on a summer thermal:

Moving down . . .
Moving down that
Lonely road
To meet my Savior
Beyond the blue

Someday, I'll go to be with
My Lord on the other shore;
As I go singing
This lonely song
To meet my loved ones,
Forever more,
Then I'll quit
Moving on.

Moving down
That dark, dark road,
To be with my Savior,
And friends forever more;
Then I'll quit
Moving on;
Someday I'll go to be
With my Savior forever more,
Then I'll quit
Moving on.

Moving down
That lonely road
To be with my Savior
Forever more;
Then I'll quit
Moving on.

The last note reverberated through the little house. E. B. relaxed like a man coming out of a trance. "Now, what about that?" he said smiling. "A man as old as me to make up a song like that?

"People beg me to sing my song a lot. Sometimes I do. And the older ones, the tears'll go to runnin' down their faces. They've asked me to sing it in church, but I'm . . . I'm just not ready for that yet. But I reckon I will be.

"Now, this song, the words of it, it's true, if you get to studyin' the meaning. I used to keep it all inside me when I was younger, but now I'm lettin' it all out.

"I wander a lot. Don't know about anybody else—but I wander. And I wander a heap a-times why the Lord let me live to be so old. Reckon I'll ever find out?"

A traditional Christmas tableau: Bringing home the tree.

Part Eight

Old Mountain Christmases

*Then we'd go out in the yard and try to see the footprints of
Santy's reindeer in the snow. And sometimes some of us were able
to see tracks. That was the great thing—to try and see the tracks.*
                                    —"Pop" Gourley

Garvel English

We were happy with that one toy.

"Christmas?" Eighty-one-year-old Garvel English raised his bushy eyebrows another notch. "Well, it used to be quite different. We only got the one toy and we were lucky if we got that," said the dean of the North Cove English clan, a family that had been in "The Cove" since Garvel's great-grandfather Gabriel bought land for five cents an acre in 1839.

Garvel and Ida made a picturebook couple, dressed in turn-of-the-century outfits as they took part in McDowell County's seasonal celebration called "Ole Mountain Christmas." Garvel wore a black coat and a fancy derby that his father wore at his wedding in 1898. Ida dressed herself in Aunt Emma Sorrell's long black dress and black bonnet. The old outfits made Garvel remember the real old mountain Christmases.

"We were happy with that one toy. Seems like children today get so much—they wouldn't be content with just one toy under the tree. Generally, we also got an orange or two, or a piece of stick candy."

Garvel was raised by his grandfather Jahu English after his father died of typhoid fever. Garvel recalled that Jahu relished the Christmas ritual, especially in the big country kitchen, with "boiled custard, coconut cake, ginger stew, and eggnog with something extra," Garvel winked.

"We always found our tree on the farm—decorated mostly with strings of popcorn we'd made. We'd have holly and mistletoe too.

Garvel and Ida English of North Cove
dressed in old-time garb for Christmas.

We'd climb for mistletoe or shoot it out." Garvel grinned at the memory of a long-ago Christmas. "I remember one time I got a red wagon. A little red wagon. It had a tin or metal body and wooden wheels with wooden spokes. I was the proudest of that. Now, that was really something."

On Christmas Eve, "we'd just take off the socks we'd worn that day and hang 'em over the mantel. Great, long, knitted wool socks they were too."

Lacie Collins

Christmas was so different . . .

Lacie Collins was crocheting intricately stitched snowflakes as she remembered the Christmas of 1905. "I'd never seen a Christmas tree or Santa Claus," the eighty-year-old Clear Creek seamstress declared.

"We went down to a little log church and school near Celo in Yancey County, and I'll never forget, I was about five and my brother was two—and my brother got so scared when he saw Santa Claus come in with his bag of candy! I'll never forget his little eyes got so big.

"Christmas was so much different from how it is now. People came and tied gifts on the branches of that first Christmas tree, and there was always firecrackers and other mischief. It was the tradition in our family to put our names on a slip of paper and put them on our plates at our place on the table. Santa Claus put our gifts on the plate: an orange, a piece of candy, some small article of clothing like a fascinator—that's a sort of a scarf.

"I never saw a stocking hung at our house," she said, speculating that the custom of receiving presents on their dinner plates was an old French custom, "since my people they came from France." It was a custom that had been carried on in her family, she noted proudly.

She remembered her first doll. "I didn't get a doll till I was twelve, and it was made out of some material that if it got wet, it'd

Lacie Collins crocheting snowflakes
for Christmas trees.

come to pieces," she said smiling. "No, Christmas was quite different from what it is today," Lacie said, her fingers dancing with the
yarn snowflakes for another Christmas tree. She had started piecing quilts when she was six, and had been sewing and stitching ever
since. Her snowflakes were her favorites. "I can almost see 'em in
my sleep," she joked.

Emma Snow Bunker

*Children of today have really missed a lot by not seeing those
old days.*

Emma Snow Bunker grew up in the Yadkin County community of
Good Spring right at the base of the Blue Ridge's ramparts at
Roaring Gap.

One of nine children, Emma recalled a busy household where
her father kept a thriving country general store and her mother
took in boarders and ran the post office. The eighty-three-year-
old Emma remembered the merry ghosts of Christmases past.
"Christmas!" she exclaimed, "Why, we children just thought that
was the best of times. We were just dying for it to come.

"In those old days my mother'd always start cooking many
many days beforehand. Mother cooked on a woodstove, of course.
She baked ten loaves of bread twice a week because we boarded
traveling salesmen coming through. There's never been a meal
eaten at my daddy's that there wasn't company. Talk about a good
cook—my mother was the best.

"Oh, the Christmas dinner was the big event. You didn't go to the
store for things like you do now. We had country ham, wild turkey,
and everything from the hog fixed every way that it could be fixed.

"We'd have a pretty little cedar tree we'd gone out and cut. And
we'd string popcorn in great, long strings that we'd drape around
it. Then we'd hang cookies with faces—all homemade, of course.

"You know, when I think about those Christmases, I think the
children of today have really missed a lot by not seeing those old
days.

"Children now get things new all the year round. And they wouldn't give two cents for what we got! We always got one nice toy—a doll or a dresser or a tea set. Then an orange, apple, or candy. And you tried to take care of what you got or you wouldn't get another one next year.

"We hung our stockings over the fireplace, and we worried a lot about Santa Claus coming down the chimney and getting burned. So Father always let the fire burn down low. We children always left Santa something out to eat when he came. I mean, it was so real to us.

"Mother ran the post office. They didn't have Christmas cards back then, but they did have postcards and folks corresponded more at Christmas time. There were so many people up above in the mountains who were so poor they couldn't afford to send their children to the four-month school, and so didn't know how to read or write. They'd come into the post office, and if they got a postcard they'd ask Mother to read it to 'em. Yes, she'd do that. And then they'd ask her to answer it for 'em right there. And Mother'd write down what they wanted to say, and then mail it right there," Emma said with a chuckle.

"Christmas was wonderful because we didn't have anywhere to go like they do now. It was *real* excitement. On the last day of school before we got out for Christmas we were treated. We'd get a bag of candy." Emma remembered the one-room schoolhouse where ages from six through thirty attended the four-month-school, as she called it. "We'd have a program with the children giving Christmas recitations and I'd always get a new dress at Christmas for that last day of school program. My mother'd make it. Oh, my mother was the best hand at sewin'. And at the school they'd have a tree we'd decorated. And music; they'd always have someone playin' a fiddle and banjo. It was something. You just can't imagine."

James Lee "Pop" Gourley

To us boys the most significant thing of the whole business was firecrackers.

"Never saw a Christmas tree in anybody's house." Ninety-six-year-old J. L. "Pop" Gourley remembered log cabin Christmases of the 1890s as being "sort of like Labor Day is around here now, but we did have the custom and practice to hang your stockings by the mantel. I guess they still do that, don't they?"

White-maned Pop, the patriarch of the Gourley family of Mc-Dowell County, remembered, "Our stockings were home-knit. Came up to your knees. We'd have one pair and wear them until the feet wore out and then make a ball outa it and play ball. But at Christmas we'd hang our stockings and get up early before dawn to see what Santy brought us.

"And then we'd go out in the yard and try to see the footprints of Santy's reindeer in the snow. And sometimes some of us were able to see tracks. That was the great thing—to try and see the tracks." Pop's deep-set eyes sparkled. "Generally we got a couple of sticks of candy, a little box of raisins, and maybe an orange—and maybe some little thing. Oh Law', that was all right—that was all we expected, just a little treat."

Then a special remembrance struck Pop. "I almost forgot—to us boys the most significant thing of the whole business was firecrackers. We almost always would each get a little pack of firecrackers in our stocking. We'd go right out in the front yard and shoot those things off—that was the chief enjoyment on Christmas Day among us boys."

Pop's most unusual Christmas memory was of a former Civil War cavalry trooper who lived nearby. "He'd get all dressed up and come riding in on a mule, drunk full of the Christmas spirits you might say, and visit the neighbors."

Pop said the Gourley log cabin, built in 1750, is still standing in Number Ten community, Cabarrus County. Pop remembered how a massive, five-foot-wide rock fireplace heated the entire thirty-two-foot-long room where the whole family of nine lived, slept and ate. "The great fireplace warmed the whole house," he said. "Supper might be cornbread and milk, with the bread cooked on a skillet by the fireplace. We were very proud that our fireplace and

"Pop" and Nora Gourley of Marion. Recalls ninety-six-year-old Pop: "We'd go out in the yard to try and see the footprints of Santy's reindeer in the snow . . ."

chimney was so big that ol' Santy could come down that chimney and didn't have to come in the front door."

Pop's mother cooked on a woodstove in the separate kitchen building adjoining the great room. He remembered the house filled with the special smell of Christmas cakes cooking. "We had chicken and dumplin's on Christmas Day, red gravy, too," he said.

"It was owing to the weather as to what we did on Christmas Day. If it was snowing we might all go out and have the horse or mule pull us around on the sled. Sometimes we'd go visiting for Christmas."

Now, some ninety years later, Pop and his wife Nora were expecting a family reunion of at least twenty folks on Christmas afternoon. There would be good eating and plenty of music with Pop leading the carol-singing as he played the organ.

Epilogue

When it was suggested that an update on the status of these people would be valuable, it struck me as a great chance to reestablish contact with so many old friends. The interviews had taken place over a span of sixteen years, and in many cases I had lost touch with the people. Inevitably when working with someone well on in years, the risk is great that death will take the person. Each of the people I had interviewed seemed to me an invaluable resource—each one a human history book. So I was actually reluctant to look into courthouse records to see who was still surviving; the folks who appear in this book are—to the very second of this reading—so *alive* for me. I didn't want to know who had died. After procrastinating as long as I could, I plunged in—and gratifyingly, two things struck me as I did my research during the summer of 1985: how many of my people were still alive and active in spite of their age, and how the stories I had received from the now-deceased were made all the more priceless and irreplaceable because their voices were stilled. *This* was their sole written record, their legacy.

As of August 1985, I had obtained the following details about the people you have met in the preceding pages:

J. D. McCormick. "I'm just tickled good to hear from you," J. D. said when I phoned him. The guitarmaker has retired now at sixty-seven, and has passed on his trade to his son, J. Douglas. The "ol' mountain man," as he likes to call himself, is still writing songs, and "playin' right smart a-music," he says. He reports that most every Thursday night he and friends make music in the living room.

Ernest Edwards. The retired itinerant photographer was interviewed in May 1980; he died September 29, 1982, at the age of eighty-four.

Reid Biddix. The man who loved his Model A Ford was seventy-four when he was interviewed. He died in May 1984 at the age of seventy-eight.

Morris Nanney. The old farmer is still going strong at ninety-four. He grew a garden again this year.

Walter Earley. The veteran scoutmaster stepped down in December 1980, but at eighty-three he is still active as a volunteer with the Scouts. At his retirement dinner, Walter vowed, "I'm not getting out of Scouting. I may die out, but I'm not quitting. If any of you ever need me, just call. I'll be there if the roads aren't blocked."

Frank Swann. Interviewed at age eighty-five, he passed the family fiddle on to his son Donald in Texas. He and Hessie celebrated their golden wedding anniversary in March 1981. On a subsequent visit, Frank allowed, "I'm a shut-in, so I love for folks to visit. But nobody visits anymore. Nossir. They don't come around to visit their neighbors anymore. The preacher comes. Howard Pullam, now he's a good 'un. I told him to hurry back. Maybe I'd let him talk some the next time." Frank laughed at himself. "I do love to talk." He died in March 1984, at the age of eighty-seven.

John McCall. The centenarian lived to be 103, dying in May 1985.

Howard McKinney. The old farmer who loved his mules had to sell them last year when his health began failing him. He lives at home with his sister Gardie.

Emmett Gray. The bearman of Lake James is seventy now and still has his trio of bruins all raised from cubs: Ella Mae, thirty-one; Sally, seven; and Sam, ten. "I still think the world of my bears," says Emmett. "Them things is something else in our lives." He still bear-hunts and takes special time with twin boys he and his wife have informally adopted. "I can be proud of my life," he says. "I got a lot to live for."

"Rhythm Willy" Shade. Seventy-seven now, the rag-popping shoeshine wizard of the City Barbershop in Marion has retired and is living at the Lake James Rest Home. Tom Harris, the shop's owner, says, "I really miss him 'round here. He's one of the finest old colored gentlemen I ever knew. There's people come by every day checking and asking about him." Tom adds, "I've talked to him and he says he's coming back just as soon as he feels a little better."

"Pop" Gourley. James Lee Gourley, Sr., died in September 1981, at the age of ninety-six.

Garvel English. Eighty-three now, he is "still going strong," reports North Cove neighbor and cousin John English.

Edsel Martin. The woodcarver with the dry sense of humor is now basking in the glow of his undisputed status as "laziest man in the county," ever since his closest rival, puppeteer Clyde Hollifield, was taken by a fine madness and started building his own house out in the woods.

Isidore Langlois. "Lang," the old jazzman who vowed to keep playing the guitar as long as he could lift a finger, is eighty-two and performing every weekend at Theo Kerhoules's lakeside Teahouse in Tryon.

Grover Robertson. The old historian, ninety-four now, still is the gadfly of Shingle Hollow; he set out a garden this year too.

Hardin's Store. Interviewed in 1979, J. Lewis Hardin, who is seventy-five now, still tends to the 100-year-old family store in Shingle Hollow.

Saney McEntire. The ninety-three-year-old WWI vet who thought he was the country's oldest living survivor, died in November 1979, three months after having been interviewed.

Laura Presnell. The old farm woman was interviewed at age ninety-four while visiting her niece in Goose Creek, McDowell County. She died in May 1984 at the American Rest Home in Forest City. She was ninety-eight.

Creed's Acme Store. The Acme Gulf Station in Rutherfordton was torn down in 1980 and is now a heating and cooling contractor's business. At sixty-five, Creed is retired. He sold the old Coxe plantation surrey with the fringe on top to Rudolph Parton. And he also sold the giant lemon and orange trees "to this boy out in the country who built a greenhouse 'specially for them—but they died anyway." Creed speculates that "plants are like people; they have to get adjusted." Maybe his trees just missed him so much that they pined away.

Joe Clark Frashier. Having taught his young'uns how to make molasses, he is seventy-eight now and has passed on the molasses mill to his oldest son, Marvin. When I phoned the Frashiers, Joe's wife, Demmie, allowed that Marvin was "going to make some right away."

Harold M. Clark. The crusty old nurseryman who loved his West Coast laurels fell into declining health in the late seventies with his dream for a revolutionary fast-growing hardwood still unrealized. He was seventy when he was interviewed in 1971.

Julia Brown and Lucy Gray. The two "awful old women," as they liked to call themselves, and who kept their neighbors on their toes, were interviewed in 1977. Julia died in August 1982 at ninety; and Lucy died in May 1985 at ninety-one.

Nelle Smith and Roscoe. Roscoe the rambunctious groundhog lived to be a venerable sixteen-year-old, dying in the winter of 1982. Nelle Smith of Gilkey in Rutherford County mourns, "He just died of old age. Just went into hibernation and didn't come out." She eulogizes, "He was quite a pig."

E. B. Hyder. Interviewed at eighty-eight, the nurseryman of Green Hill in Rutherford County seems unstoppable at ninety-four. He's still working daily, tending his trees and plants. Witnesses report recently seeing E. B. out manning a garden tiller with a younger man standing by just watching.

Tommy Lee Robbins. The retired cleaner who dreamed of running a trolley car in Spindale died in May 1976. He was eighty-seven.

Sam "Handy" Haynes. The peanut man of Spindale, interviewed in 1972, lived to be ninety-one years old. He died in May 1981.

Charlie Lance. The ninety-four-year-old retired mail carrier of Fairview in Buncombe County was the last person interviewed. When I talked to Charlie in June 1985, he was living quite contentedly at a rest home right on the route where he used to carry the mail by buggy and horseback. When I was taking his picture, I couldn't get him to smile, until I realized he was blind and couldn't see I was bald. "Bald as a baby's butt," I announced as

Charlie began to smile at the notion. Then I told him about a home-grown hair-raising remedy one old farmer told me about: take sheep manure and mix it with kerosene, make you a good paste, and then plaster it on your head. Wear it around all day in the sun till it gets good and stiff. . . . By this time, old Charlie Lance was laughing—and I took my picture.

Aunt Lena Dellinger. "Nannie," the matriarch of her clan in Crossnore, Avery County, was feted by the little village with an open house on her ninetieth birthday. Practically all of Crossnore turned out for the affair in July 1980. That Christmas "the best Christmas gift of all," she said, was one of music: five grandchildren clustered around her bed and sang songs to the old woman. She died in March 1981.

Joe Henson. The ebullient Christmas-tree grower of Avery County is reported to have given up smoking at age sixty-three. And he's still full of fun and jokes. The other day he said of his Christmas-tree patch, "Some of that land up on the hill is so poor that a rabbit has to pack a lunch to get across!"

Doc Watson. Now an international star, Doc tours with his son Merle, and commands respect and draws rave reviews wherever he plays his blazing six-string.

Berthy Byrd. Berthy, seventy-three now, and Charlie, eighty-three, were on the square again last year at the Burnsville crafts fair making their apple butter. I visited with Berthy during one apple-butter-making session in November 1982, at Jim and Jewell Warrick's farm in Relief, Mitchell County.

Aunt Kate Burnette. Ninety-one now, and spry and energetic as ever, Aunt Kate still cuts her own firewood. "I made an awful good garden this year. My ol' deep-freeze is about full," she declared proudly when I called her. "I am thankful to the good Lord for my health. Somehow I just seem to keep a-goin'. And the Lord bless you too!"

They keep the old things that never grow old.

—**Carl Sandburg**

Runnin' on Rims has been composed in Scotch
No. 2 with Goudy Old Style display on a
Mergenthaler Linotron 202 by G & S Typesetters
of Austin, Texas. The book was printed and
bound by Dai Nippon Printing Company of
Tokyo, Japan. It was designed and produced by
Joyce Kachergis Book Design and Production of
Bynum, North Carolina.